IDEAS UNLIMITED

How To Run A Successful
Suggestion Scheme

IDEAS UNLIMITED

James McConville and Andrew Wood

THE INDUSTRIAL SOCIETY

THE UNITED KINGDOM ASSOCIATION
OF SUGGESTION SCHEMES

First published 1990 by
The Industrial Society
Robert Hyde House
48 Bryanston Square
London W1H 7LN

ISBN 0 85290 4762

Typesetting by Barnes Design + Print, Maidenhead.
Printed and bound by Billings Ltd., Worcester.

CONTENTS

10 DOWNING STREET

LONDON SW1A 2AA

THE PRIME MINISTER

More and more companies are coming to know that the ideas and imagination of their own workforce represent a powerful resource which can bring great benefits for the company as a whole.

Employees are well placed to make suggestions for improved working methods and new ways of approaching problems which they confront daily. Their valuable ideas not only help companies save money and run more efficiently but also lead to better staff communications. Suggestion Schemes are an excellent example of employee involvement in action. I commend the United Kingdom Association of Suggestion Schemes for its contribution to this important area and send my best wishes on the occasion of its Annual Conference.

Margaret Thatcher

July 1989

FOREWORD

We hope that this book will be of value to anyone interested in suggestion schemes, whether managing a scheme, thinking about setting up a scheme, or wondering how to re-vitalise an existing scheme. Many organisations have yet to appreciate and develop the full potential of the latent creative and innovative talents of their employees at all levels. The rewards can be substantial and they are there to be shared by everyone concerned. Of these rewards the most obvious are the financial benefits, which can be very significant. However, the immediate monetary benefits are secondary to those generated through the creation of better teamwork and a sense of common endeavour.

We believe that ideas springing from within the organisation represent the most frequently neglected source of creative opportunity. The potential can be as important as that derived from any other source and needs to be treated just as seriously by every organisation genuinely in search of innovation.

Senior managers, planners, market researchers, investment analysts, and consultants all play an important role in innovation and the development of future strategy. Development is, after all, an essential part of their respective jobs. But what about the hidden reserves of talent which exist amongst other employees of the organisation? Why should creativity be restricted to those who happen to have it specifically written into a job description? No one is better placed than the individual employee in an operational area to observe the opportunities and the problems which arise in the day-to-day relationships with customers, suppliers and people on different sides of departmental boundaries.

We therefore hope to demonstrate the potential which exists for encouraging, rewarding, and implementing good ideas arising from within the organisation. In purely financial terms we estimate that the potential savings in the United Kingdom are of the order of £300 million per annum.

This estimate is given credence by surveys carried out in North America, which show that savings of $2 billion per annum are being achieved. As further evidence we have the practical experience of our own companies, Industrial Society members and of other members of the United Kingdom Association of Suggestion Schemes. Information about UKASS services appears in Appendix I.

The value of suggestion schemes is increasingly recognised and the Association was pleased to receive a message from the Prime Minister which is reproduced on page vi.

Our aim throughout this book will be to focus on the concepts and the practical issues involved. The book has been written to complement the *Ideas Unlimited* video produced by BBC Enterprises, but it will also provide a useful source of reference for those who have not seen the video.

We would like to thank everyone who has contributed to this book. In particular we would like to thank Karen Edwards of the BBC who provided the inspiration for the original *Ideas Unlimited* series and Bryn Brooks who produced the programmes. Both Karen and Bryn have made a tremendous contribution to the launch and subsequent promotion of the United Kingdom Association of Suggestion Schemes.

Our other partner is The Industrial Society. Special thanks are due, firstly, to Jean Balcombe and her team for all the work undertaken in the launch and administration of the Association, secondly, to our publishers Gilles Desmons and Beth Beisel for all their patience. Finally, we would like to thank the members of the UKASS team and all the organisations who have contributed to the section on individual suggestion schemes.

James McConville
Andrew Wood

SECTION I

THE CONCEPT

By James McConville

INTRODUCTION

Why have suggestion schemes?

Some years ago the Chief Executive of a major British company was asked what value he placed on good ideas originating from within the organisation. The answer was swift and positive, "We place tremendous importance on ideas from our staff, in fact our staff suggestion scheme has been operating for more than 20 years."

A subsequent survey amongst staff revealed that less than 50% knew that a suggestion scheme existed and, of the remainder, few believed that it operated fairly or had any direct relevance either to their jobs or to their personal prospects. The suggestion scheme concerned was effectively dead and had probably been so just a few years after it was introduced 20 years ago. Incredibly, analysis of the ideas put forward revealed that some had lain unanswered and even unacknowledged for as long as five years! It was hardly surprising that the scheme lacked credibility with the staff. Yet the Chief Executive had been content to believe that in this regard the company was at the forefront of modern business practices.

Fortunately, this cautionary tale has a happy ending. Following a major review the backlog was eliminated, the flow of good ideas increased by a factor of seven, and 95% of staff questioned in a more recent survey listed the suggestion scheme as the natural focal point for all good ideas lying outside immediate job responsibility. Furthermore, the company is now benefitting from savings of many hundred of thousands of pounds per annum, and the employees with winning ideas are well-satisfied with their rewards. Interestingly, the question which prompted the Chief Executive to take a fresh look at a very old concept came from a member of staff during a brainstorming session to come up with good ideas on how to improve its flagging company performance.

It took the company a combination of difficult times, a searching question, and a responsive Chief Executive to wake up to the potential of a scheme designed for the business environment of the 1990s — not based on the well-intentioned but now completely out-moded and paternalistic designs originating from the 1920s or 50s. We are now witnessing the re-birth of an old concept which can begin to tap the hidden assets of talent and imagination which are too often forgotten, ignored or simply stifled. The prize is a leap forward for teamwork, partnership and involvement.

The changing image

Why do we need a book about suggestion schemes? After all, they have been around for a long time. Indeed, the British Navy claim to have had a scheme in place since 1869, although no doubt putting forward ideas for radical change was a great deal more hazardous than it is today.

In the business world suggestion schemes were first introduced as a "modern" practice nearly one hundred years ago. Therefore they must be about as relevant to the business world of today as the original Remington typewriter. It seems that we have a problem!

However, the original concept of the typewriter as a means of producing the printed word has actually not changed. Instead new technology and applications have continually updated its form and image, i.e. from manual to electric, to word processor to personal computer. In a similar way suggestion schemes have undergone significant changes in concept and application. In this case the response has been to new developments in the management of human relationships. This coincides with the recognition that competitive advantage can only be maintained by continuous change and innovation, hence a need to seek out and develop creative ideas from every available source. Perhaps our problem is that, unlike the old typewriter, the suggestion scheme has continued to be stuck with its original label.

Too many organisations have decided that because suggestion schemes have been around a long time, then they must be out of date and irrevelant. We can say with confidence that a predictable fate awaits any suggestion scheme which retains old-fashioned methods of operation as well as an old-fashioned identity. Yet the most successful of today's suggestion schemes continue to retain the best elements of the original concept but are unrecognisable in terms of method of operation and appeal. The challenge therefore is to create a fresh and positive image in the marketplace, that is with the employees, and at the same time to demonstrate the substantial benefits to be derived from new approaches.

All in the name

Although traditional descriptions continue to be used by most organisations, we would like to see the demise of the label "staff suggestion scheme" and with it all the implications of paternalism and divisiveness. Why "staff" and not "team"? Why "suggestion" and not "idea"? Why "scheme" and not "system"? If we are to change its image then perhaps we also need to change the brandname.

"Ideas Centre" is our preferred generic title. Some people will no doubt argue that "Innovation Centre" is more appropriate, but we like the more simple label which everyone can understand. We believe that the title "Ideas Centre" more accurately reflects the process which encourages creativity and teamwork, and which translates ideas from concept to reality. The specification for the perfect "Ideas Centre" would require that it be a friendly and efficient facility designed to encourage, nurture, develop, implement and reward good ideas arising from within the organisation. The "Ideas Centre" should also provide opportunity for people who are themselves creators and innovators.

The "Ideas Centre" is a concept which offers opportunity in many areas for the visionary organisation. There are numerous sources of creative ideas available to every organisation but few are developed to their full potential. "Ideas Centres" can help to improve significantly the chances of success.

Many companies have in fact already created their own centres for employee ideas and at the same time have introduced brandnames for the products, e.g. Winning Lines – British Rail; Brainwaves – British Airways; Bright Ideas – Eastern Electricity. The most successful companies no longer tend to retain any of the words contained in the old label of staff suggestion scheme. Furthermore, all appear to have recognised that this is an area of opportunity requiring a unique combination of skills in both the fields of human relations and innovation.

CHAPTER 1

THE OPPORTUNITIES

The immediate response of most people when asked about opportunities and benefits is that suggestion schemes save organisations money and at the same time provide financial rewards for those who come up with the ideas. Whilst this answer is correct, it is by no means complete. More importantly, there is no reference to what is now generally accepted to be their primary benefit. It is therefore useful at this stage to produce a checklist of opportunities.

The primary opportunity

The most important single opportunity deriving from a modern, well-managed suggestion scheme lies not in financial returns but in the contribution which is made to achieving greater involvement and commitment by everyone. A good scheme should play a valuable role in improving communication and in promoting and enhancing a common purpose. Employee involvement is essential for survival in a world of accelerating change and increasing competitive pressures.

It is undoubtedly true that a scheme is likely to achieve the greatest success when operating within a culture which has already adopted an open style of management with good communications and a "Putting People First" attitude towards the employees. Indeed the chances are that even an up-to-date scheme would fail, like many of its predecessors in earlier years, if introduced into an organisation with rigid hierarchical structures and strict dividing lines between employees.

The opportunities for the suggestor

Monetary

The prospects of a welcome financial return will certainly remain an important motivator for the person who comes up with a good idea. These days even a minor suggestion can be worth between £10 and £50. Financial improvements resulting from good ideas are typically rewarded on the basis of a percentage of the amount saved, over a twelve month period, with a range from 10% to as much as 50%. With some suggestions producing financial gains which can be reckoned in tens or hundreds of thousands of pounds, then clearly the incentive is significant. Even though there is usually an upper limit, in large organisations the reward can be as much as £25,000.

Personal satisfaction

The financial benefit, however, is by no means the only reward for the successful suggestor. Many people who have received awards claim that the satisfaction of achievement is of equal if not greater importance. No doubt the degree of satisfaction correlates with the time and effort expended on development.

Recognition

Finally, the successful suggestor enjoys the recognition of achievement which is expressed by a proud family, friends and colleagues, and the Board and senior management of the organisation. This counts for a great deal and is best rounded off by a special presentation of the award and a certificate by the Chief Executive. It is all the better if the husband or wife is there to enjoy the occasion – it could well be one of the major highlights of a career. The scheme itself benefits at the same time from the opportunity to promote a successful story.

The opportunities for the organisation

We have already discussed the primary opportunity for the organisation in terms of the contribution to teamwork. Clearly, the second most important benefit is likely to be generated by improvements in financial performance. Ideas which result in cost reductions within a technical environment have traditionally been the main source of financial improvements resulting from suggestion schemes. Indeed in the past some schemes have been restricted to the shop floor activity, presumably in the belief that good ideas simply don't arise in an office environment.

While it remains true that the majority of winning ideas in terms of value still tend to be of a technical nature, the actual flow of ideas from other areas is frequently greater these days. Many organisations, of course, have no technical operations at all other than in the information technology side of the business. However, such organisations often have excellent schemes such as those to be found in central government, for example the Inland Revenue, the Ministry of Defence and the Department of Social Security. The latter is achieving savings of over £6 million per annum, which is 17 times the cost of running the scheme, including awards of over £100,000.

Financial improvements are not restricted to cost-saving ideas. Increasingly, significant contributions are being made from revenue generating ideas which improve customer service or enhance the product in some way to create a more attractive package. The travel-related services industry is an outstanding example of a sector which is proving to be a very fruitful ground for good ideas through suggestion schemes.

Size of organisation — Is it important?

"Suggestion schemes are probably only relevant to organisations with more than 500 people."

True or false?

To answer this we need to distinguish between the mechanics and the concepts — what are suggestion schemes really all about? Under one definition the mechanics prevail and schemes are seen as no more than convenient bundles of administrative systems and procedures devised to process internally generated ideas by the most efficient means. If we take this line, then economies of scale must clearly establish some lower limits on the viability of formal schemes. Thus in a unit of just a few hundred people it will obviously not make sense to try to replicate, even on a small scale, the complex procedures and infrastructures which are appropriate for the giant organisation.

The conceptual view is that "suggestion schemes" are catalysts and energisers which encourage teamwork, involvement and reward for good ideas. Given this definition the scope and applicability becomes very much wider and the size of unit and the operational mechanics are of secondary importance. The successful formula is simple:

- all ideas are welcome
- everyone can put forward ideas
- we will listen to all ideas
- we realise that some ideas will not work
- but every idea deserves a cheer
- and a forum for ideas can be useful.

This formula works successfully in many small organisations where the leadership provides encouragement, opportunity and reward. The mechanics only become critical when the Filofax can no longer cope. Our own response to the proposition set out earlier is that it is false — suggestion schemes are a concept which is applicable to any organisation irrespective of size.

CHAPTER 2

INGREDIENTS OF SUCCESS

The scheme

There is considerable evidence to show that a number of factors determine whether or not a scheme is successful. These will be developed fully in Section II, but a quick summary is useful at this stage.

- Visible commitment and support at top level. This encourages a climate of innovation, and ensures that the management chain responds positively and promptly and supports promotional activity, for example by presenting major awards. The top level commitment obviously starts with the Board and the Chief Executive but also needs to include all senior managers.
- Eligibility for the scheme includes people at all levels together with simple methods for submitting suggestions.
- Assessment procedures which ensure that all ideas are reviewed positively, i.e. a "why not?" approach.
- Efficient administration and systems to acknowledge ideas immediately, to put them forward for assessment, to ensure that evaluation is properly completed and to monitor and report on performance in respect of overall flow and turn-round of ideas.
- An approved budget to support the administrative resource, promotional activity and the cost of awards. One of the principle reasons for the failure of schemes is inadequate resourcing based on an assumption that they can be run as a spare-time activity.
- Marketing and promotional plans which treat the scheme as if it were a product destined for the outside marketplace with all that this entails, including brand name, logo, advertising, publicity and special promotions.

- Rewards that are fair and consistent within a framework which is clearly understood by all potential participants. The requirement is to set out the basic rules for entry and to explain the evaluation procedure in a way which is precise and simple to read and understand.
- Teamwork and partnership to promote the scheme and evaluate ideas, with involvement wherever possible by staff representatives.
- The creation of a network of assessors and "champions" of good ideas, drawn from people who have a positive approach to new ideas. Enthusiasts are to be found in every organisation and they will usually find the time required voluntarily. These are the innovators and change-makers who respond to the "fun-factors" of business life.

Obviously this can by no means be an exhaustive checklist, but most of the key ingredients for success are included, based on the experience of the leading practitioners in this particular field. The list should help to identify areas for improvement in existing schemes and in planning for the launch of new ones.

Positive attitudes

There can be no doubt that the flow of creative and innovative ideas is significantly greater in organisations where the suggestion schemes themselves are designed, run and managed in a creative and innovative environment. Here a positive attitude prevails in every aspect.

Contrast this approach with the characteristics of some suggestion schemes which have failed or are currently faltering. A feature which is frequently symptomatic of a negative approach is a tangle of rules and procedures which are seemingly designed to cut the chances of a good idea being successfully implemented by 50% before it has even been submitted! Such rules and procedures are the natural product of a bureaucratic organisation. They invariably tend to be written in ways which circumscribe and restrict rather than encourage freedom of thinking and action.

Voluminous rules and procedures to regulate every aspect of behaviour are regrettably still to be found in many organisations, in both public and private sectors. These are the organisations which, probably for reasons of insecurity, retain rigid internal structures with strict hierarchies and dividing lines between departments and between people at different grade levels. Typically, the schemes in such organisations will be called the "Staff Suggestion Scheme", so as to acknowledge the delineation required by the culture between "The Management" and "The Staff".

Listed on the following page are examples of the negative approach as extracted from various rulebooks.

- "No suggestion will be accepted if it relates to the place of work of the staff member."
- "Suggestions will be immediately rejected if they are considered not original or not practical."
- "No appeals will be considered."
- "The name of a suggestor will not be revealed to a management assessor."

If an organisation has procedures like this, then the best thing that can happen is for them to be thrown away and a fresh start made. Guidelines are, of course, required. Make them simple and easy to understand. Above all ensure that every statement is *positive and encouraging* and always come out into the open with the names of people involved unless there are very exceptional reasons.

Winning teams

But writing positive guidelines is only one aspect. As is usually the case the important issues relate to the people involved in running the scheme. Here is a checklist of points to consider in team selection.

- Is the team responsible for running the scheme selected from people who are themselves natural creators and innovators? Avoid the bureaucrats!
- Equally, has the network of assessors also been selected from people who are positive thinkers?
- Has any form of training been developed for those involved, even if only by way of a half-day workshop?
- Is the encouragement of new ideas included as one of the standard performance measures for every manager?
- Is there an appropriate way of recognising and rewarding the effort and achievement of those involved?

We find that organisations with highly successful schemes have usually addressed some or all of these questions.

The winner

What makes a winning suggestor? What personal characteristics are most likely to be found amongst people who have winning ideas?

We put these questions to a group of suggestion scheme managers and they came up with the following list of personal attributes:

- creative
- imaginative
- observant
- innovative
- determined
- hopeful
- involved
- positive.

We then put the same questions to a group of winning suggestors, and once natural reticence and modesty was overcome, they put forward a very similar list but made three further points:

- sometimes luck can be involved
- thinking up a good idea can be fun
- everyone can be a winner.

The last point is the most important of all. Full marks to the suggestors for coming up with a better list than the managers! All these points are extremely important and need to be properly understood if a suggestion scheme is to achieve its full potential. We will look more fully at how these characteristics affect individual motivation and performance in Chapter 4.

Winning ideas

Where do good ideas come from?

Good ideas come from Woolworths! The winner of the first BBC "Ideas Unlimited" competition was Mick Rowlerson of British Airways. Mick is fond of telling how his brainwave suddenly occurred to him while out shopping with his wife on a Saturday morning in Woolworths. What he saw was that a simple flap-wheel on the hardware counter costing just a few pence could be adapted to slip through the narrow neck of an aircraft strut rather like putting a ship into a bottle. This idea is continuing to save many thousands of pounds every year and, at the same time, has added to air safety. The problem which Mick solved was one which had defeated the best engineering brains.

The point to be made is that good ideas can come from almost anyone, in any place. Furthermore, it isn't necessary to be a technical wizard to be a winning suggestor. As already indicated, important new sources of good ideas are being discovered away from the traditional technical areas. Ideas designed to improve customer service are one such growth area for suggestion schemes. Employees who are in daily contact with the customer have a unique opportunity to observe the realities of how the latest marketing or sales campaign is working. They are the eyes and ears of the organisation.

We are now seeing a significant switch in approach, away from a focus restricted to "what went wrong?" to address the issue of "what does the customer really want?" The opportunity for good ideas is tremendous and many organisations are now seeing the flow of customer service ideas overtaking those from the traditional technical areas. There are, of course, often problems in the evaluation of such ideas, because it may be difficult to determine how much additional revenue is directly attributable to the new idea. The answer is to be fair and positive, always giving the benefit of the doubt to the suggestor. To do otherwise endangers the potential flow of good ideas in the future.

Problems in search of ideas

Most suggestion schemes operate on the principle that the suggestor is expected not only to put forward an idea but also to identify an issue or problem to which it can be applied. But how is a suggestor always to know that a problem exists?

The reason why more ideas are not forthcoming is, of course, that the people who could possibly help do not know that a problem exists. How can they be aware of a need to address particular problems or seek new opportunities if there is little or no communication?

Setting out issues and problems is a positive approach which can open up many new areas of opportunity. This should not be dismissed too readily on the grounds of confidentiality.

Greenfield areas

The majority of ideas will probably continue to come from people who see ways of doing things better. However, what about ideas which relate to things which are totally new? The idea could be an entirely new process, a new product or perhaps a new market. The flow of ideas in this category is usually small since it is relatively more difficult to be creative in greenfield areas. Yet there is often significant untapped potential in this area, and this should be encouraged.

Ideas which do not have a quantifiable financial value

In this vital category there are many excellent examples of good ideas which produce improvements both for the organisation and for its employees. These will include ideas which address health and safety matters, new approaches to environmental issues both inside and outside the organisation, ways of easing the daily transition from home to the workplace, e.g. why not have a creche? An idea on any of these could represent a major contribution, but they are likely to be placed into an "intangible benefit" category and, all too often, will not receive fair recognition. In fact "intangible" is entirely the wrong label when the results are there for all to see and enjoy. Ideas in these categories are definitely tangible – the only problem is that they are less easy to measure in financial terms. Avoid the trap set by an awards formula which is too rigid and only works when results are easily measurable in strict financial terms.

CHAPTER 3

MEASURING PERFORMANCE

Because a suggestion scheme can easily lose momentum, it is essential to assess its effectiveness constantly. Various measures of performance can be used, but the most important relate to the number of ideas received, the number awaiting assessment at any time, the number of ideas which are implemented, the value of awards made, and the overall financial gain for the organisation. The performance measures will usually be presented for the organisation as a whole on a monthly basis and are often broken down to show results by individual departments. We will look at each of these key measures in turn and comment on the sort of performance to be expected.

Number of suggestions received

The standard measure used here is the number of suggestions received per 100 employees. Based on the UKASS and Industrial Society 1988 survey completed in the United Kingdom the *minimum* acceptable rate of entry is five suggestions per 100 employees per annum. Anything less than this should be taken as an indication that the scheme is in trouble probably because of poor publicity, unattractive awards or general loss of credibility. Action should be taken to isolate the reasons for low involvement, followed by the development of a re-launch package.

Ten suggestions per 100 employees can be regarded as satisfactory and may provide a useful initial target for the launch of a new scheme. However, the most successful schemes are achieving rates of 25 or more ideas per 100 employees per annum.

Number of suggestions implemented

The number of suggestions implemented is usually measured as a percentage of suggestions received. An adoption rate of 25% is probably average. Even so, three out of every four ideas submitted are being rejected! It is for this reason that the more enlightened organisations treat every idea as a good idea and make some form of award.

If the rate is very much less than 25% then something is clearly wrong – either the quality of ideas is very poor or, more likely, the rulebook is too restrictive, obliging the assessors to reject nearly every idea. Whatever the cause, expect the flow of ideas to lessen as people become disillusioned about their chances of becoming winners.

If the rate is well above the 50% level, then congratulations are in order because the organisation obviously has an imaginative workforce as well as an excellent suggestion scheme.

Suggestions awaiting assessment

The number of suggestions which have been received but have not yet been assessed is a vital indicator of the performance of the scheme's management and administration. All suggestions should, of course, be acknowledged as soon as they are received. The real test is how long it takes to say whether or not the idea is to be implemented and what the size of award is to be. Ideally all suggestions should be cleared within a week, but often this is simply not practical. Clearance of all suggestions within one month is a more realistic objective for publication, but even so there will still be legitimate exceptions. Some ideas may well require an extended period for development and testing. In the aircraft industry, for example, there may also be a requirement to obtain approval from the aviation authorities to gain certification for a proposed modification. It is therefore difficult to set hard and fast rules and much will depend on the nature of the business concerned. It is, however, most important to produce regular reports showing the number of suggestions outstanding and for how long, for example more than one month, more than two months and so on. This report should be broken down by department and should go to the Chief Executive.

Value of savings and increased revenue achieved

Most organisations set annual targets of revenue saved due to their suggestion scheme. There will always be an element of uncertainty because the incidence of major winners cannot be predicted. For this reason the target should not be overambitious. The main reason for the published target is, after all, to promote interest and to publicise success.

In the United Kingdom, the average financial benefit derived from implemented suggestions was £1,250 based on the survey. Some organisations, however, achieve as much as £5,000. In reporting performance the key statement should show the total figures for the month plus the accumulated result.

Costs of awards, promotions and administration

The average financial award given in the United Kingdom is currently less than 10% of the financial benefits achieved. It appears, however, that this figure has been reduced by the inclusion of numerous "incentive" awards of around £25 which are given for near misses. Most major ideas are now attracting awards ranging from 10% up to 50% of the financial gain achieved, although, regrettably, there are cases of suggestors who have literally saved millions of pounds and received only a few hundred pounds by way of awards. Higher awards are usually made for ideas which have an ongoing as opposed to a "once-off" value. In terms of reporting it is usual to report monthly actual and accumulated figures.

Costs of administration are one of the budget's few fixed elements and are obviously determined by the size of the organisation. It has been estimated that for a properly run scheme one administrator is required for an organisation with between 500 and 1,000 employess, two for between 1,000 and 5,000, three for between 5,000 and 10,000.

The financial summary — costs and benefits

Using realistic figures based on the survey, the method to develop a cost/benefit summary is illustrated below. The example is based on an organisation with 4,000 employees.

Number of employees	4,000
Suggestions received at 10 per 100 employees	400
Suggestions adopted at 25%	100
Average financial return per adopted suggestion	£2,000
Total gross financial return	**£200,000**
Cost of awards at 12.5% of financial return	£25,000
Cost of administration – two people	£30,000
Cost of special promotions	£5,000
Total costs	**£60,000**
Net financial return	**£140,000**

In this example costs of £60,000 per annum support a return of £200,000, i.e. a return of 3.3 times the cost. If the Financial Director comments that this is ten times more than from a normal investment and therefore highly suspect, then refer to the experience of members of UKASS. In fact the *average* gross financial return is between five and ten times the running cost. The only condition for success of course is that the scheme is properly managed in line with the recommendations set out in Section II.

CHAPTER 4

CREATIVITY AND INNOVATION

What do we mean by Creativity and Innovation? The words are clearly fashionable with some organisations and appear with increasing frequency in business journals and management textbooks. But why do we think it relevant to discuss creativity and innovation in a book which is all about suggestion schemes?

In this Chapter we shall be taking a closer look at the *processes* that are involved in the origination of good ideas and in the translation of these ideas into practical and rewarding applications. This, of course, is very much the task of the suggestion scheme manager. A sound appreciation of the underlying processes is important for day-to-day operations and when designing and planning for optimum performance of a scheme.

Improved understanding of these processes will also contribute to better performance by the organisation as a whole because the principles involved apply to every aspect of the business, particularly at the points where change and new thinking is required. Within this wider perspective, a suggestion scheme is only one of many areas of potential application, but it can act as the catalyst for developments elsewhere.

Definitions

Creativity and innovation are terms which are often applied too loosely and are sometimes used as though they were synonymous. Below are more precise and relevant definitions. It is useful at this point to provide a definition of the Ideas Centre which was referred to in the Introduction.

- Creativity is the process of exploration, research, imagination and lateral thinking, which firstly recognises a potential opportunity, and secondly proposes possible ways to exploit the opportunity, usually in conceptual terms only.

- Innovation is what it takes to translate the opportunities and solutions identified through the processes of creativity into reality by establishing the resources, accountabilities and timing required for successful implementation.
- The Ideas Centre (sometimes described as the Innovation Centre) is the catalyst and focal point which ensures that optimum results are obtained from the processes of creativity and innovation. The Ideas Centre will promote, encourage and reward creativity. It will also critically evaluate proposals and, if viable, gain approval in order to facilitate and sponsor the programmes and resources required for implementation.

Within the framework of these definitions the role of the suggestion scheme and its component parts should be apparent. The suggestors themselves are creators who are, potentially, the initiators and major contributors to the creative process.

The assessors, line managers and project teams — who evaluate good ideas and turn them into reality to achieve cost savings; to improve revenues, customer service, or health and safety; or to launch new and profitable ventures — are the innovators. They are the principal contributors to the innovative process. Within this process, wherever possible, the suggestors themselves will make a further contribution through continuing involvement.

If an organisation wants to achieve the optimum potential from the creativity and innovation of its employees, then the cornerstone must be the suggestion scheme itself.

This is the theory. But how do we identify and measure the elements of the creative and innovative processes in order to create a successful Ideas Centre?

Requirements for successful creativity and innovation

Most people are naturally creative. Think of the many creative activities which people become involved in when away from work, ranging from personal computing, to home improvements, craft skills, sporting adventures, and so on. So why aren't more good ideas put forward and actioned in the work-place? Why do some organisations seem to have a far better success rate than others, acquiring reputations for being at the forefront of positive and profitable change through innovation?

To answer these questions, it is necessary to consider the conditions under which organisations and the people within the organisations operate. What makes them tick? In other words, what cultural and organisational characteristics are likely to determine the difference between success and failure?

Below is a simple model to illustrate the processes and the key elements found in organisations that are successful innovators. Most of the points should now be familiar since they are also found in most successful suggestion schemes.

Managing for Creativity and Innovation

CULTURE WHICH
ENCOURAGES CREATIVITY

+

CREATIVE PEOPLE

+

THINKING TIME

=

GOOD IDEAS

+

PROPERLY RESOURCED
IDEAS CENTRE

+

INNOVATIVE MANAGERS
PROJECT TEAMS
TECHNICAL AND FINANCIAL RESOURCES

=

SUCCESSFUL INNOVATION

This model suggests that good ideas are more likely to be produced in a culture which encourages creativity, recognises creative people, and allows time for the creative process. Needless to say all this does not happen by itself. It requires leadership and vision to bring about and to sustain the right conditions.

Managing the organisational requirements

A checklist of necessary conditions for successful innovation can be developed. This will include factors which relate to the organisational structure and some which relate to the selection, training and development of the people involved.

- Visible commitment to creative change and innovation at top level.
- A climate which encourages creativity and innovation and recognises individual and team commitment.
- Innovative managers who are willing to take sensible risks and to delegate effectively.
- Open and constructive communications with a sharing of information across internal boundaries.
- Ideas Centres with the dedicated resources required to produce results.
- Development funding for start-up situations.
- A toleration for failure as the quid pro quo for the encouragement of risk-taking.
- Flexibilty in organisation structures to remove barriers and provide for freedom of access.
- Management targets which require specific actions geared towards the encouragement and development of creative ideas.

Managing the people-related requirements

Organisation structures will not work unless the people involved are properly selected, trained and motivated. Successful organisations tend to invest in the following.

- Assessment centres and selection techniques to identify people with the dispositions and skills which make for creativity and innovation.
- Career development programmes, which include elements specifically designed to promote awareness of opportunity through innovation.
- Training and development for managers in the techniques and skills required for managing creativity, innovation and change.
- Training and workshops for all employees to encourage teamwork and awareness of opportunity.
- Performance systems which provide meaningful rewards both for individuals and teams for innovative achievement.

Obstacles to successful innovation

Factors most likely to mitigate against successful innovation include:

- Rigid organisational structures and specialist functions.
- Distance and lack of access to the decision-maker.

- Innovation seen to be the prerogative of others, i.e. management elite and the specialists.
- Investment procedures which are averse to risk-taking.
- Resistance to any change in the status quo.
- Inadequate presentation of the business case.
- Conflicting priorities and lack of time to consider new projects.
- Lack of fit with the corporate goals.

While these are major obstacles, top-level commitment can successfully surmount these problems through investment in management-of-change programmes and the introduction of new approaches to people-related issues.

Sources of good ideas

Suggestion schemes represent only one of many potential sources of good ideas. A comprehensive list of sources might also include the following.

- Research and development
- Other specialist planning and research functions
- Directors and senior managers
- Quality Circles
- Competitors
- Suppliers
- Customers
- External research establishments
- Government

The chances of success

Work undertaken some years ago on research programmes in the UK showed that, for all ideas which were treated seriously on first selection, some 1,400 were needed to produce an added value of £1 million per annum.

The most recent UKASS and Industrial Society survey shows similar results. These indicated that, on average, 1,000 *accepted* ideas are needed to produce savings of £1 million. Accepted ideas are defined as those which are actually implemented, around 25% of the total received.

The chances of receiving a winning idea in the major league, worth over £100,000, are therefore not unduly poor, for example, 18 short-listed entrants to a UKASS Industrial Society competition had between them achieved savings of over £2 million. Furthermore, there are several instances of savings of over £1 million resulting from an individual idea.

Managing for major winners

How are ideas with major financial potential captured and taken forward for successful implementation? How do we minimise the chances of missing the really big winning idea by not giving it a fair hearing?

The solution has to lie in the establishment of properly resourced Ideas Centres. The only way to minimise the risk of losing a major winner is a positive evaluation process, adequately resourced, which always takes a 'why not?' approach.

Once potential major winners have succeeded in passing the critical evaluation hurdle, resources will be required to translate them into action. These may be manifested in a variety of ways depending on the idea's specific needs, e.g. technical or marketing expertise, time and facilities for further development, financial support, project management support and so on. Again, they may be provided by the Ideas Centre itself but, more likely, they will be found from within the relevant line functions.

Measures of successful performance

A variety of measures are relevant when considering the assessment of performance. They fall into three main categories relating to:

- the work-load involved
- the people involved
- organisational behaviour.

The first category, concerning work-load related measures, is the simplest to introduce and involves purely practical considerations, such as how long it takes to respond to an idea, how many there are in the pipeline and so on. These will be considered further in Chapter 7.

The second category concerns the people involved. Standard performance reporting structures must include measurements which relate specifically to innovative skills both in terms of the application of the process and the way in which the people are managed and motivated.

Finally, there is the question of organisational behaviour. Is the company a highly creative performer, or a high performer in terms of innovation? Perhaps it is both, perhaps neither. Where would it fit in the model shown on the next page?

An organisation which is a poor performer in terms of both creativity and innovation is unlikely to survive unless supported by public funds. An

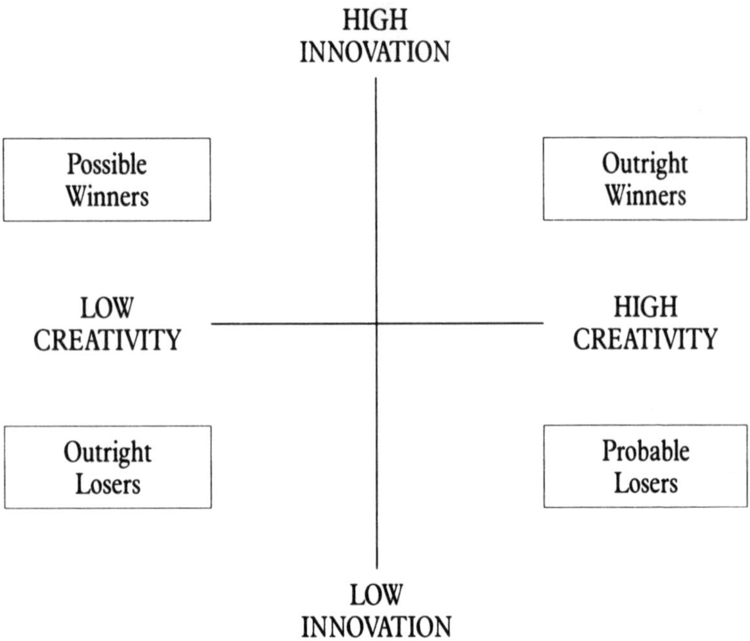

organisation which is highly creative but which cannot innovate is also a probable loser because others will take and copy the ideas.

A possible winner, however, is the highly innovative organisation. Creativity is not of absolute importance because other people's ideas can always be copied and mistakes can be avoided. Thus the ability to achieve fast and efficient implementation can often overcome the disadvantage of being late in the field.

The outright winner will always be the high-performing organisation in terms of both creativity and innovation. The challenge for these organisations is to maintain this position. To do this, inevitably, an innovative approach will be necessary.

Success depends ultimately on a combination of techniques designed to build the right environment and to select, develop and motivate the right people.

SECTION II

THE PRACTICE

By Andrew Wood

CHAPTER 5

STARTING A SCHEME

If we have made a convincing case for having a scheme, then it is important that a professional view is taken of starting the scheme. Too many organisations launch a poorly thought out scheme only to see it flounder a few months later with considerable ill will. At times consultants have set up schemes centred on marketing the scheme, but have left the organisation poorly resourced to deal with the new ideas. The result, again, has been considerable loss of credibility.

Research

The first step must be research, just as with any other management project. There are several ways to carry this out: calling in consultants who are experts in this field or speaking to similar organisations that have a suggestion scheme already in operation. Both The Industrial Society and UKASS have much information, and a series of seminars and workshops are held at various locations at frequent intervals. Section III is devoted to case studies of existing schemes, which provides interesting preliminary research in comparable industries. The video available from BBC Enterprises, The Industrial Society and UKASS will also give you a good understanding of the task involved. A checklist follows of questions and advice for a champion of good ideas on how to get started.

- What are the likely costs/benefits of running a new scheme? Use the outline described on page 16 to work out a first estimate based on the number of employees in the organisation.
- Make a list of six people from different parts of the organisation who you believe are likely to be enthusiastic. They are probably some of the change-makers of the organisation, i.e. people who are themselves

always looking for new ideas and willing to experiment. Avoid the bureaucrats and people for whom change represents a problem.

- Ask them for their ideas, perhaps arrange a visit to a local company which is recommended as having a good scheme and/or get in an adviser from UKASS or The Industrial Society.
- Start to develop an informal survey of opinions, opening with the question, "What happens to good ideas in our organisation?"
- Talk informally to some staff representatives and get their views on the current situation.
- If the organisation has a scheme which isn't working, then analyse the reasons why, using the checklist of ingredients for success in Chapter 2.
- Talk to the marketing experts – hopefully there will be one in your team anyway. Ask them for ideas on how to launch/re-launch a scheme.
- Identify someone to arrange the required administrative support. Update the initial cost/benefit estimate to include all the new thinking.
- Finally, prepare an outline of the launch plan. Only an outline please because your next task is to sell the idea to the Chief Executive. You must include his or her ideas as well.

Remember that your objective is to arrive at a position where the Chief Executive "owns" the idea just as much as you and your team.

Presentation of case

The sponsor or 'champion' of a new suggestion scheme must start with the presentation of the business case, a statement setting out the research results and laying down options. A well-researched and well-written report presented to the Board or Chief Executive — backed up with the video and statements from other companies — is the recipe for success. The report must include all the advantages that are to be gained from running a scheme: financial, the building of teamwork, the identification of talent, creation of a cost-conscious workforce, and the role that any scheme can play in the communication network. It is a mistake to focus solely on the financial benefits, as this emphasis detracts from the overall concept. Experience shows that organisations which concentrate only on the financial benefits tend to have a less successful scheme.

A good business case will demonstrate how similar organisations have benefitted from schemes and will conclude with a series of options. The report should be clear, however, on the way the system is to take shape. Although it is important to have input from the Board and the Chief Executive, by this stage there should be a clear idea of the options available.

The report should be fairly straightforward and not too detailed. If a detailed report is put forward at this stage, the proposal might be rejected for the wrong reasons. Obtain support to launch a suggestion scheme first, then agree on details afterwards.

When the report is presented and accepted, the first essential to a successful scheme should be achieved: top management support.

Detail of system

Once the support and commitment of senior management is obtained, determine the detail of how to proceed. It is essential that support be visible. Thus plans should include senior managers to maintain top-level commitment. Also, at the initial establishment of the scheme it is essential that the likely workload is assessed and a realistic workforce and budget is allocated.

The detailed way to administer a scheme is discussed in Chapter 7; the general order and principles to follow in launching a scheme are set out here.

Budgeting

Unfortunately, many schemes are run without a proper budget, which results in dependence upon other parts of the organisation for funding. It is essential to provide a budget which has an allowance for personnel, advertising, publicity and equipment, e.g. word processors. Also, a reasonable estimate should be budgeted for awards based on the ideas to be received. However, every scheme should have the backing of the organisation to fund awards to any level, as the benefits generated will more than match this amount.

The budget, therefore, should produce a financial benefit estimate for the first three years based on the predictions of ideas submitted. A good test of the initial figure is to determine how much is to be spent on all the constituent elements and then multiply this by five to give the likely savings. The only other cost will be that of awards and this will depend on the proportion of payback to the suggestor that is to be made. A typical budget is likely to include:

Staff Administration Costs	• total salary bill • expenses to visit other sites
Office equipment	• VDUs, printers, photocopiers • filing cabinets • desks • office stationery
Publicity material	• launch leaflets • posters • submission forms • free gifts • video
Advertising	• artwork and cost of adverts in the house journal • certificates for winners • photography costs at special events • special event costs
Awards	• estimate of likely annual amount • special prizes (e.g. Best Idea of the Year.)

The above checklist relates to the first year costs, and many of these costs will not continue in future years, e.g. provision of office equipment. It must be remembered, however, that growth of the scheme should be provided for if the anticipated success materialises.

Taxation considerations

Award winners of ideas put through suggestion schemes in the United Kingdom enjoy a special tax concession. The concession is only available to organisations with properly constituted suggestion schemes that comply with particular requirements relating to eligibility.

If all the conditions are fulfilled, then an individual award winner can receive up to the first £5,000 tax free, only being liable to pay tax on anything above this figure. This is obviously an extremely valuable concession and most organisations in the UK have made sure that their schemes are constituted so that this benefit is available. The key requirements include the following:

- The scheme must be properly constituted and open to everyone.
- Ideas must relate to activities which are outside the suggestor's job responsibilities.
- The suggestion must have been developed in the suggestor's own time.
- Ideas can be put forward by several people and not just one individual. However the tax concession is only available once, i.e. several people jointly putting forward an idea will share the concession of up to £5,000 tax free.
- The tax free limit for initiative awards is £25.

These conditions clearly mean that ideas put forward through, for example, a quality circle will not be eligible for the concession from a suggestion system. This is one of the reasons why, in the UK, suggestion schemes and quality circles are regarded as being complementary but not integratable.

Given this position it is clear that great care must be taken in structuring the constitution of the scheme with particular attention to the question of eligibility. It should, however, be noted that none of the conditions outlined above precludes other forms of incentive payments which will of course be liable to tax in the normal way.

The Notice on the Extra Statutory Concession is reproduced in full in Appendix II. This must be used as the definitive reference for setting up the constitution of a scheme, together with advice from your local tax office. The brief outline set out above is not sufficient.

Eligibility

Who should be eligible ?

The answer to this question is very simple: everyone. In fact we know of several examples where the Chief Executive or the Managing Director has successfully put forward good ideas! This may be somewhat unusual but all credit to them for entering into the spirit of the initiative and for demonstrating personal interest and involvement.

A clear message about eligibility for everyone can be very important as a means of overcoming some common preconceived notions, for example that only technical ideas are likely to succeed or that managers and supervisors must naturally have other and better ways of developing new ideas. In fact putting forward ideas through a suggestion scheme is often a useful way of getting round the natural resistance of encroaching into another individual's territory.

It is also important that there is no apparent discrimination between different parts of an organisation. Therefore, everybody should be allowed to submit their ideas. Indeed the Inland Revenue guidelines on taxation of awards rules that everyone must be included.

What suggestions are eligible?

While many organisations do not give rewards for ideas from people whose responsibility it is to effect that change, the Inland Revenue only requires that these suggestors do not receive an award free of tax. Do not exclude these suggestors or, more importantly, their ideas too soon. In fact, one organisation positively encourages ideas from people in this way.

When should an idea be considered to be within an employee's own duties? Generally there are two guiding principles.

The first principle applies to employees in a non-managerial or supervisory position. In this case, could the suggestion be adopted by the suggestor without reference to either a:

- manager
- supervisor or
- technical department?

If the answer to all these is NO, then the idea cannot be considered a part of the suggestor's own duties and an award should be made.

The second principle should be used for ideas from employees in supervisory or management positions of the organisation. The issue is less clear in these cases, but the basis of the decision depends on whether the suggestion could be adopted by the suggestor as stated above and in addition:

- would the suggestor be open to criticism by not coming forward with the idea?

If the answer in all cases is NO, then the idea cannot be considered part of the suggestor's own duties and an award should be made.

However, the case may not always be so clear when suggestors put many hours of their own time and resources into the development of the idea. In these cases the practice is to reward suggestors, but at a lower level of payment which reflects the relationship with their own duties. Each case should be looked at individually with the employee's own manager who must remain the final arbiter on all 'line of duty' issues.

In setting eligibility rules no idea should be rejected before its evaluation. This is the most important criteria. Evaluate all ideas fully before looking at who it is from. Also, let employees know the rules on eligibility. Too often suggestors are unsure of their qualification to enter, and if they are unsure they might not submit their ideas.

Confidentiality

In the most successful organisations everything associated with the suggestion scheme is open. Ideas are written on cards that circulate in open letters through internal mail, and evaluators are fully aware of suggestors' names and can talk to them to get a deeper understanding of their ideas. Some organisations have ideas written in a book so that other employees can add their own thoughts to the original idea in order to develop it.

In contrast, there are, regrettably, still some organisations where every individual is assigned a number and every evaluator is hidden by a faceless committee. Confidentiality may appear to protect the suggestor, yet it is usually insisted on by managers who feel threatened by the flow of ideas. Managers' apprehension of an open scheme is a serious aspect to consider when determining the level of confidentiality in a scheme. In organisations seeking to revitalise an ailing scheme, changing to an open scheme may prove to be one of the most difficult, but most important hurdles to overcome.

We do recognise that some employees are so inhibited, or unsure of their own ability, that to reveal their identity would actually deter them from submitting an idea. This is unfortunate, but it is something which will have to be recognised in drawing up the groundrules for the scheme. However, the more open the system the less likelihood of it being viewed with suspicion, especially by the employees.

Style of scheme

There are various options open when starting a scheme. Consideration must be given to determine which is the most suitable for a particular organisation.

Traditional approach

In this method the ideas are encouraged from individuals but nothing specifically is done to create a corporate identity amongst suggestors. The approach may be favoured by organisations with isolated employees. Individuals may still contribute to the two following styles of schemes which encourage more group activity.

The club approach

In this system employees become members of a club. This creates a greater sense of belonging to the group. As a result, members (employees) are more likely to feel a sense of identity with their organisation.

There are two ways that this could be organised. One is to include everybody in the club as soon as they submit an idea; whilst the other is to restrict membership to those suggestors who have been winners and had an idea adopted. We make no firm recommendation either way, although the latter may give a greater sense of achievement.

Club members may be given a badge, but it could provide many other benefits to give members a feeling of importance.

The team approach

In many organisations ideas are identified with groups, or individual sections of the workforce are arranged in teams. In some cases, teams compete for a special prize based on either the number of valid ideas put forward or on bonus points being awarded for the value of adopted suggestions. When running a competition all must be aware of the rules and the team sizes should be adjusted by the weighting of the points. An annual award can be given in the form of a trophy, or a cash payment can be given to the group or to a charity of their choice. This method can be helpful in increasing participation in the scheme.

Submission of ideas

Specially designed forms on which suggestors may make their submissions are an essential element of the scheme. However, it is unwise to exclude ideas that do not arrive on the standard form. The idea may only merit two out of 10 for presentation, but it could well have 10 out of 10 for content. Always remember it is content that will be adopted, not the presentation.

There are many different types of submission forms. The precise detail must be left to the individual organisation. In some organisations where an open system is practised a card is used. The suggestor writes the idea on one side and the other is used for the evaluating officer's comments. This card is signed by both and the suggestor and evaluator may approach each other if they are unable to determine facts or understand each other.

This system will not work if people wish to remain anonymous or if the organisation continues to refuse to disclose the identity of evaluators (such organisations are most unlikely to have a successful scheme).

Ideas are often sent out photocopied to evaluators. If this is the case remember not to use paper of such a colour that it is difficult to read the idea when copied.

The types of forms and their styles are summarised on page 35.

What forms should include

To be effective, design forms to encourage the submission of ideas. They MUST:

- be clearly laid out
- leave a large space for the suggestor to write down the idea
- allow the suggestor to entitle the idea
- allow the suggestor to say what operation the idea concerns
- have a space for the suggestor's name
- have a space for the suggestor's normal work address
- show where the idea should be sent (or better still either provide an envelope or devise the form in such a way that it folds into an envelope)
- include the phone number of the administration team where help may be obtained
- include the rules
- make it clear that only one idea should be entered on each form
- inform suggestors to add extra sheets for lengthier ideas
- use plain English.

They SHOULD:

- incorporate guidelines for submitting ideas
- include the organisation's corporate identity
- use the suggestion scheme motif or logo.

They COULD:

- outline the areas where ideas are needed
- have a section which evaluators may complete.

TYPE OF ENTRY FORM	BENEFITS	DISADVANTAGES
Any piece of paper	• suggestor may write idea at any-time and anywhere • ideas do not have to be tailored to fit a specific size or form • will not deter people put off by forms	• can fail to include vital information (e.g. own name) • may not be aware of any rules • may not know where to send idea
Specially designed paper entry form	• ensures all necessary information given • aids filing in the administrative unit • rules can be clearly shown on form • address for submission may be included and the form may fold into a self addressed envelope • may incorporate the evaluation form • may include corporate identity or team logo	• can be reason for not sending in idea if supply depleted • can deter entry if forms have to be obtained from a distant location • forms can deter people
Specially designed card form	• all those in above except special envelope will be needed • more robust record than above	• all those above

Written submissions

Once the form has been designed and produced, establish clearly how it should be submitted. The process needs to encourage the transmission of ideas in writing. The options available will depend on the size of the organisation, but they are likely to be:

- suggestion box(es)
- via managers
- via supervisors
- via internal post
- via electronic mail
- personally submitting to team.

We have never been great supporters of boxes. Doubtless there will be those who know of a successful operation using boxes, but we have yet to come across one. Boxes must be emptied every day at every location and they must be kept polished and free of dust. They must not be capable of having liquids spilt into them when suggestors rest a coffee mug on them. Experience shows that sooner or later, for whatever reason, the box is not emptied, and as a result the scheme falls into disrepute.

In all organisations managers and supervisors should encourage suggestors to participate both by helping them phrase their idea and by pointing out items which need solutions. Therefore it is a useful addition for ideas to be submitted via managers and supervisors.

The submission of ideas by internal post, providing the address is clear, will most likely be the simplest form available, especially for schemes in which the suggestors wish to remain anonymous.

Finally, submitting ideas in writing is not the only way that ideas could originate.

Verbal submissions

The verbal submission of suggestions can be very effective, as several organisations have found. Many schemes encourage suggestors to call at the suggestions office and discuss their idea with the team. Many ideas would have fallen by the wayside if this approach had not been adopted. In addition, people can send in ideas by using an answerphone. Many people do not find it easy to express their ideas in writing, but the use of the answerphone or the telephone overcomes this. Experience has shown that the answerphone has been particularly useful for suggestors who work on a shift system and are at work when the suggestions team is not present. The important thing to remember with an answerphone is to ensure that the tape is transcribed onto an entry form at least once every day.

The rules

There is a requirement by the Inland Revenue that the rules of the scheme be published. Even without this requirement we firmly believe that it is essential for rules to be freely available. The rules must be written in the simplest form so that they can be understood by all levels of staff. There are many ways that these may be published, but one excellent method is to use the reverse of the submission form.

One of the most important aspects of the scheme is how the rules are written. They must be both clear and positive. Rules that use negative words like 'can't', 'don't', 'will not' and 'shall not' can counter the most persuasive of publicity. If appeals are allowed, and we strongly recommend that they are, then the rules should explain the procedure and method by which they are made and adjudged.

Administration, evaluations and rewards, and marketing

This chapter has dealt with the basic issues that should be considered when launching a scheme, starting from the presentation of the report to the Board, through the preparation of a budget and the consideration of how the ideas should be presented.

Several other issues must be considered before you are in a position to launch the scheme.

- How will the scheme be administered?
- How are the ideas to be evaluated?
- On what basis are rewards to be made?
- What sort of marketing and publicity should the scheme be given?
- How should the scheme be refreshed once the novelty has worn off?

In the chapters that follow these issues will be dealt with in more detail.

CHAPTER 6

MARKETING THE SCHEME

Before embarking on marketing the scheme, it is vital that the scheme is viewed as if it were a product to be launched into an external market. Therefore, it is important that a clear understanding is reached on the objectives of the scheme and a vision statement should be prepared which sets these out.

From these objectives will follow:

- expectations of benefits both intangible and financial
- what research is required
- who can help
- what are the constraints
- what are the cultural/environmental influences
- what is the market
- what is the product
- what is the 'Brand Name'.

Determination of objectives is an important prerequisite of determining the marketing strategy. The strategy should decide on:

- advertising
- public relations
- sales force
- promotions
- sponsors
- publicity
- launch.

The final issue is to make things happen, and this will result in an action plan that establishes target performance measures. We shall now deal with each of these issues.

Setting the objectives

The establishing of objectives is important because it will determine the style of marketing that will be undertaken. Thus a scheme that seeks the total involvement of employees will concentrate on generating ideas from everybody, and will have a different emphasis to a scheme which has an objective to generate either large cash savings or safety improvements.

Market research

Before embarking on the launch, research should be carried out. The research could determine people's expectations, and may identify a training need to help people think creatively. If a scheme has previously existed, then it is essential that all employees' perceptions of the scheme are determined. A sample survey should test understanding of eligibility, award levels and method of submission. The facts which are revealed will highlight shortcomings which need to be corrected.

Research may reveal that a pilot scheme ought to be launched in a specific area to measure systems.

In Chapter 3 we outlined a number of key performance measures. These can be developed to provide the initial launch objectives and the essential management information on performance. However, they are not generally sufficient and need to be supported, at least on an informal basis, by ongoing research into awareness and attitudes. Occasionally this may justify an independent attitude survey, but it is usually more convenient to approach the matter through a group discussion or workshop, asking "What do *you* expect from the scheme", if one doesn't exist; or if one does, "What do *you* think about the scheme? How can it be improved?" Such sessions do not even need to be specially arranged and can often fit into a forum which also addresses other issues. As well as general points, questions could include some which are aimed at specific areas of concern, for example:

- How many people know about the scheme and how to enter? Is the award system understood?
- Why don't we get many good ideas from the finance department? What is the secret of success with the engineers?
- What suggestions do you have for improving the scheme? Is the turn-round rate now acceptable?

Much valuable information can be gathered in this way. Because it involves participation the process also helps in promoting the scheme.

Who can help?

The opportunity should be taken to gain help and support from departments with the skills needed to promote the scheme. The Marketing Department is the natural one to involve, but the Public Relations people can be helpful too. It is useful to ensure that you get everyone on board who may be able to assist.

Are there constraints?

It is certain that there will be some constraints which will need to be borne in mind. The most obvious will be the finances available within the budget, but there will probably be others which need to be considered.

Examples to be thought about are: the literacy levels of the employees; the attitudes which may exist towards a scheme; any management fears; and any workload constraints. To a greater or lesser extent, all will influence the style of any marketing campaign.

What are the cultural or environmental influences?

Every organisation has its own culture even if it is not particularly perceptable. There may be a very open culture where managers converse using first names, by contrast, other organisations insist on always using Mr., Mrs., Ms, etc. Some organisations are happy to make verbal agreements, whereas others will insist on everything in writing.

There can be physical influences too. The organisation that has a one-site factory is able to award different items than one spread throughout the country. Posters may be difficult to display to a workforce on the move, compared to one that is static. These are issues to bear in mind at the planning stage.

The market and the product

Marketing the scheme is an essential ingredient of its success. The scheme should be viewed as a product, and as with any other product it needs to be promoted. The advantage here over any normal marketing exercise is that the market is a closed one comprising all the organisation's employees and there is no requirement to seek new markets in which to promote the product, only in new ways to market it. (An exception could be the extension of the scheme to retired staff, customers or contractors.)

To market the scheme, the Scheme Manager needs to identify ways to reach all employees. However, the scheme will need marketing in two different ways: to employees who will participate and to managers who will encourage their employees and be convinced themselves of the value of the scheme.

Even in a small organisation where the Scheme Manager could speak to all employees on a regular basis, it is still essential to carry some if not all of the element of marketing the scheme presented in this chapter.

If the market is the entire staff, the product is the commodity outlined in the objectives of the scheme. So the objective may be "to encourage everybody to participate in making improvement ideas" or alternatively it could be "to obtain benefits of £200,000". These two objectives are shown to illustrate that a different style of marketing may well be run to suit each. It is very important that before deciding on the style there is clarity about the product and the market.

A brand name and a logo

Do you think that 'Ginger Nuts' would sell as well if they were called 'Edible, dark brown, hard, ginger-tasting biscuits'? So why do so many organisations insist on calling their scheme 'The XYZ Machine Tool Staff Suggestion Scheme'? Why not a brand name? Most of the recently introduced schemes are now marketed under one.

Get a good name — a competition can even be run to think of one.

Branding

A brand name which identifies the scheme is important. If it is possible to link the name with the organisation's business activities, or to capitalise on an image already in use, this can cement a greater sense of corporate identity. There are already many good names such as 'Ideas Club', 'Ideas Unlimited', to name but two. Section III provides a selection of details on individual schemes.

Logo

It is a good idea to consider the use of a logo with which the scheme may always be associated. There are a number of ideas which could be used: a symbol, cartoon, or friendly animal. The animation of a familiar logo can be one extra marketing tool which may be used on several occasions. The case studies in Section III reproduces the logos of some organisations' schemes.

The specifics

The pre-planning stage should now be complete and a specific action plan drawn up.

These may include:

Awareness

The most important role of marketing is to make people aware of the product. It is vital that the entire workforce is made aware of the scheme. This will help people who may have been reticent to try submitting an idea or suggestion before the scheme's existence. How this initial awareness is conveyed to employees is dependent, to a large extent, on the type of employment they are engaged in and where they are located. Therefore a hundred employees all working from home would be apprised of the scheme in a different way to a hundred who all work in one building.

Posters

The launch poster should be the initial one in a series of posters which are exhibited throughout the first year. Posters should be kept simple; too many words will not be read. It may be very tempting, especially at the launch, to include as much information as possible. Don't do this. Aim to introduce the logo and the scheme. Simply say that ideas are wanted and where to send them.

Posters are more effective if they are bright and colourful. If there is a house style this can be incorporated into the poster design.

Posters need to be re-issued on a regular basis to be effective. This should include periods when the notice-boards are empty to draw maximum attention to the appearance of a new poster.

Leaflets

Some organisations rely more upon leaflets issued to each employee than posters. However, leaflets can be effective but it is a good idea to compliment them with posters. Leaflets give a greater scope for publicising details of the scheme. They can, for example, include considerable information about particular ideas which are wanted. Leaflets may be printed on both sides and can incorporate a submission form. Posters and leaflets may adopt a particular theme. These could be based on different ways of performing tasks in a quicker, cheaper, or neater way; energy saving ideas; ideas for making an operation safer; ideas to eliminate waste; or ideas to make an item larger or smaller. Posters and leaflets can announce special prizes and competitions run either to encourage a specific type of idea or to announce a special prize.

House magazine

This will be the best medium for keeping everybody within the organisation up-to-date on the progress of the scheme. The Scheme Manager should make a friend of the Editor. However it would be wise to make sure that an advertisement which is aimed at promoting the scheme appears in every issue for as long as is necessary. If this has to be paid for then provision must be made for it in the budget.

Articles about the scheme should be encouraged and details of all winners together with other successes should be fed regularly to the Editor of the House Magazine. If these details are not forwarded, then it is unlikely that an article will appear. A regular column showing all winners is the ideal.

At the launch it will be particularly helpful if the scheme is given a prime position in the magazine, for instance the leading article. This should not be too difficult if the launch has been timed properly and editorial staff have been kept informed of progress. The Managing Director or Chief Executive may be keen to feature in this article promoting the scheme.

Newsletters

Larger organisations have found that a special newsletter or newsheet about suggestions can be very effective. A good rule about this is to make them bright and chatty. Don't make them look too like an office circular or people may not read them. Include photographs if possible, showing previous winners, good ideas, and suggestors having fun at ceremonies. Try to ensure that the newsheet is not boring and unattractive. It can therefore have a smattering of cartoons and jokes if they can be found on suitable subjects. (Don't be tempted to joke about some of the more outrageous ideas you have received — it may deter suggestors if they feel they could be thought foolish.)

Articles can be written helping people to formulate ideas, and interviews with suggestors saying how they thought up ideas may be useful.

If yours is a small organisation, don't be discouraged. There is much that can be produced on a few brightly coloured sheets. Perhaps you may care to have additional copies of *UKASS News* to circulate to employees.

Video

Depending upon the size of an organisation the use of video should be considered. The credibility that this can lend to the scheme, especially if a famous personality appears in the video, makes it well worth investing in this medium. If the organisation is to make a personal video related specifically to that organisation's suggestion scheme, then this can give even greater credibility and understanding.

The video must be shown to people in an organised way. If a method of team briefing is already established, then this can be utilised. If this is not the case then a special showing will need to be arranged. It is desirable that the video is shown to the workforce in the presence of managers who can explain the scheme and answer any questions.

A video for the workforce should demonstrate to employees the types of ideas that are wanted and show examples of successful ideas that have been presented before. It should show the rewards that staff may receive for their idea and convey the sense of pride that all suggestors feel when their idea is adopted.

The BBC Enterprises video produced with the help of The Industrial Society and UKASS is ideal to demonstrate the value of suggestion schemes to Chief Executives, co-ordinators and employees. It will prove particularly useful to smaller companies who may find a corporate video too expensive.

Mementos

Many organisations give away mementos in certain situations and this is usually a good idea. Mementos can cover a whole range of items, from basic pens, pencils and rulers to clocks, torches and larger gifts. They should be available when employees submit ideas and at special promotions. The type of memento/gift given will depend on how it is given away. For example, if displays promoting the scheme are mounted, then the size of the items need be of no major concern. However, if the items are sent to employees, then thought needs to be given to wrapping and despatching the memento.

There can be two objectives to giving mementos. The first is to provide an advertising boost to the scheme and a reminder of the scheme in the workplace.

The second is to provide a thank you to the suggestor. They are not necessarily complimentary.

The mementos which will encourage suggestions and will also indirectly help the scheme as a form of advertising are of relatively low value, so it is likely that the item will stay in the work location. An item of greater value may be taken home. An item taken home will not meet the objective of giving the scheme an advertising boost.

If, however, the objective is to give suggestors an item they will feel is prestigious, then a different item should be awarded. A cheap plastic mug may stay at work; a china one would be taken home.

With the first objective the items may be awarded to everyone as they make a suggestion, regardless of the quality of the idea. If the memento is more valuable only those ideas that have reached a predetermined quality standard may qualify.

It is important that mementos are suitable for the whole workforce. This means that they must be equally attractive to all types of worker and to both sexes. A very poor choice of gifts does little credit to the scheme and the scheme's image may be harmed.

Organisations that only award ties, or give smart leather desk diaries, could well be presenting gifts that men in offices may prefer but would be unsuitable for women working on a lathe. A range of gifts is the obvious solution, but it must be remembered that offering people a choice involves a greater degree of administration, both writing to suggestors to ask their choice and then receiving and acting upon their reply.

Introduce the team

In a scheme that covers a multi-site operation, or is comprised of many thousand employees, it is important that the operation is not viewed as remote and faceless. In either of these circumstances it is a good idea to identify the team members and members of the committee so that they may be approached about the scheme. Suggestors will find it easier to approach someone whose name they know and have some knowledge of. Thus if a team's members are featured in a poster or leaflet, and a brief resume of their background included, then the employees may be able to select the member that would best be able to understand their idea.

Special prizes

Special prizes may be awarded to suggestors and this can feature in promotional material and at events to publicise the scheme. These prizes may be awarded for all ideas on specific subjects or they may be presented for meritorious ideas. Some organisations have a special Award presented whenever an idea reaches the required standard. Other suggestion schemes award cars for ideas which reach a certain level of saving, say £200,000.

The objective of making awards of this nature is to encourage yet more suggestors to participate in the scheme. An award which captures the imagination is a memorable one, and good publicity surrounding the award will ensure that the objective is achieved, and encourage the success of the scheme.

Showcase

There are several organisations which operate on a single site and an advantage over the multi-site ones is that a showcase may be maintained in the workplace, preferably the dining or resting area. Articles which may be selected as awards can be displayed, and these items can be taken from the case and shown to other workers. More importantly, the display of the goods presents the awards in real terms and employees know they actually exist. This can act as a great incentive to think of good ideas.

Other publicity

At a launch, especially at a one-site operation, another way of drawing attention to the new scheme would be to display announcements or 'teasers' about the scheme all over the building, i.e. not restricted to notice-boards or bill boards. The scheme announcements can be displayed hanging in corridors, or even pasted to windows to be visible from outside as employees arrive.

Pre-Launch

Before the scheme is launched it may be a good idea to distribute advance information to the workforce such as leaflets or posters of the 'Coming Soon' variety, which could reveal half the logo. These need to be exhibited for at least a week before the launch and removed the day before.

Personally distributed leaflets may be more effective in multi-site organisations where the control of posters may be more difficult to achieve.

With all the above issues firmly organised and the planning stage complete, it is time to launch the scheme.

The launch

The launch of the scheme can be compared to that of a new car. The principles remain the same.

For the same reasons that a garden centre should not be launched in the winter months, the launch should not be undertaken until the personnel who are to run the scheme are in place and all the launch material is available. Once all this is established it is important that the time of the launch is carefully planned. For the greatest potential sales it would not be sensible to arrange the launch at certain times, for example, just prior to and during holiday periods, during industrial disputes or when another corporate initiative is being launched. In these circumstances it would be better to wait until a more appropriate time.

The launch should always be seen as a major initiative within the organisation. Go for a 'Big Bang' launch; beat the drums everywhere, but be prepared to deal with the initial onslaught of ideas.

Ongoing features

Most of the marketing actions outlined above may be repeated at regular intervals; thus every few months it is worthwhile taking down the old poster and replacing it with a different one.

Additionally, various other activities may be built upon on an ongoing basis.

Report on scheme success

It is good practice to prepare a report containing facts about the scheme and distribute it to all the organisation's managers. The Scheme Manager should make regular reports to the Managing Director on the progress of the scheme against the targets set and a considerable amount of information will be available. The report may be on a yearly basis and cover all aspects of management information. Participation rates should be measured and compared between different types of employees. The speed of evaluation can also be compared and the number of ideas that have been adopted by different evaluators may be presented.

Displays

In the multi-site operation it may be several months between awards of significant size being made at a specific location. If this is the case the scheme can quickly be overlooked. To overcome this a mobile display can be produced and exhibited at locations on a regular basis. The display should have different leaflets available for staff to take and feature previous success stories, demonstrating how easy it is to have a good idea. A display which is accompanied by members of the team who are able to talk about success stories is more effective than the free-standing display but this will depend upon the size of the team and the budget available.

Special draws

A very good way to increase the awareness of the scheme is to run free draws whereby all who submit ideas may be entered into the draw. One advantage of this type of promotion is that it is a good measure of the number of people who are reading posters or other publicity material.

The procedure is to issue a poster or special leaflet announcing the draw.

This could take place over a three monthly period with several winners every month. It is more effective to go for several small winners than to concentrate on a large award. The total of any draw money must be included when assessing any award for taxation purposes referred to earlier. Consideration should thus be given to just one star prize with many small prizes. A popular attention grabbing phrase to use in a spring-time draw could be 'Let us pay for your holiday', whilst a draw run in the autumn could feature 'Christmas Hampers'.

The great advantage of draws of this nature is that people who would not otherwise take notice of scheme publicity are attracted and are more likely to be tempted in the future when they do have a good idea. It may be that the ideas submitted to gain entry into the draw are often of a lower standard but many good ideas which have been lying dormant will surface as a result of the attraction of the draw. We counsel caution to ensure that the law relating to this subject is honoured.

Certificates

It is a good idea that the suggestor always receives a certificate or perhaps a badge. This should be recognised within the organisation so that other employees are keen to obtain one. The photographs taken at a presentation ceremony will be enhanced by the inclusion of a certificate. The type of certificate awarded may vary, perhaps depending on the category of suggestion. All ideas that are adopted should be accompanied by a certificate signed by the Chief Executive or Managing Director to emphasise the importance with which the contribution is seen. The effect of a personally signed and calligraphied certificate enforces the belief that the suggestor is important, and that the certificate is not simply a pre-printed administrative document.

Presentation

The most effective way of presenting an award to the successful suggestor is in the workplace before all the other potential suggestors. Here everybody can take part in the ceremony and will recognise that a fellow employee has received an award and made a contribution to the future success of the organisation.

This approach should be used at every opportunity and in all schemes where confidentiality is not enforced. The presentation of all awards should be through a manager. Whilst we do not favour schemes that run with anonymity rules, we do feel that if the scheme does operate this way then this gives an opportunity for the suggestor to reveal their identity and have a presentation.

The motivation deriving from the presentation of an award cannot be over emphasised and its effect can be measured by the flow of ideas from the location of the successful suggestor.

Sporting events and sponsorship

Many organisations have sports facilities and run competitions and tournaments. Often a relatively cheap way of obtaining extra publicity for the scheme is by awarding the trophy in a particular tournament. For example, support can be given for the Inter-departmental Sea Angling Competition where the prize money is quite small and yet supporting posters may publicise the scheme by saying 'angling after an award? Then send your good idea to . . .', or alternatively, 'get onto another winning line with your good idea'. There are many possible ways of taking advantage of this type of sporting event.

Suggestion scheme sponsorship of, say, the organisation's football team could be well worthwhile if the organisation has a team competing against other local companies, though this is not advisable for internal competitions. The benefits are the regular appearance of photographs in the house magazine and the active involvement of the scheme in other activities within the organisation.

Calendars and Christmas cards

A calendar is always an essential part of the office or factory – one produced to promote the scheme will serve as an advertisement for the whole of the year. It can be far more effective than a poster, which has a short life-span, as people will constantly refer to it. The size and scope of the calendar will again depend on the budget available to the organisation. It may be a sensible idea to have a different calendar for evaluators and suggestors. One interesting fact that has emerged from past experience is that it can be cheaper to produce a customised poster style calendar than to have a prepared calendar overprinted.

An excellent way to make suggestors feel important is to send each of them a Christmas Card. If it can be signed by the suggestions team that will be even more effective. The calendar could also be used in this way if it is not to be generally released.

External publicity

This may be gained in several ways and it is important to remember it is a bonus as no fees are paid for publicity. This being the case it is more difficult to obtain.

Newspaper articles

An article in the local paper showing a member of the workforce receiving an award is a valuable boost to both the employees in general and the organisation's standing within the community. To be featured on the BBC's 'Ideas Unlimited' programme is an even greater boost to the entire workforce. It is also worth a considerable amount in terms of sales and the credibility of the organisation.

The amount of publicity that can be gained through newspaper articles is well worth the effort involved. If the organisation has a Public Affairs Department they must be fed with the stories of all the winning presentations as they will usually be able to have these stories published in the local press. If there is no public affairs organisation, then a series of simple rules will need to be followed. Rarely will a local paper attend an event like the presentation of an award, so the Scheme Manager must be prepared to write a 'press release'.

When writing a press release include:

- a strong, positive title
- a simple story relating who, what, why, where, when and how
- a report written in short, sharp, simple sentences, avoiding too many commas
- avoid unnecessarily long words
- introduce the most important facts first, the less important ones later
- check that spelling is correct, especially names
- always date the press release
- always double space and type
- always include a daytime telephone number and contact name
- a photograph if possible — action shots are far more likely to be used than a line up of individuals (black and white in preference to colour).

Annual report

Every public organisation produces an Annual Report which usually covers different aspects of the organisation's achievements, and the successes that are created by the scheme should find an entry in the report. This will demonstrate that the organisation holds the scheme in high esteem and will give great credibility to it within the management, the workforce and the community at large.

Monitoring

In talking about the performance of a scheme earlier, we said it was essential that the pulse be taken regularly. It is essential to keep the marketing effort at full strength, continually capturing the employees' imagination and promoting high participation. We have already explained how monitoring should take place and when it may be sensible to go for a re-launch.

The Re-launch

At some stage every scheme is likely to need some form of rejuvenation. If the scheme has simply lost some of the initial momentum, then a re-launch is perfectly appropriate. However, a re-launch can be counter-productive in some circumstances and we would like to offer some important advice. Never attempt to re-launch an out of date scheme which has lost all credibility – bury it, mourn it, forget it! Then launch a new scheme under a new name, new image, new management, new style!

Writing off a loser and starting again is one of the fundamentals of effective marketing strategy. Too often out-of-date schemes have failed for the second time around because of a failure to shake off the associations of the old scheme, such as paternalism, divisiveness, and apparent unfairness.

Re-launch action should be reserved for schemes which are performing reasonably well but which are in some danger of losing momentum and in need of stimulation to sharpen interest and awareness.

Warning signals which indicate a continuing levelling off or down-turn in performance should be the starting point for considering whether a re-launch is needed. A re-launch must be regarded as a *major* event and should not be confused with the regular promotions, competitions and changes in advertising which are the principle way of maintaining momentum on a month-to-month basis. A re-launch every two years is probably about the optimum frequency, taking into account the additional costs which will be incurred.

The principle considerations involved in a re-launch are:

- It must be presented as a *major* event and marketed accordingly. In particular, care is needed to ensure differentiation from normal advertising and publicity, i.e. it must not be seen as yet another special promotion.

- There will be a requirement to restyle and freshen up the logo and the key slogans, perhaps with new designs, new colours, new typeface. This is likely to involve some investment in new posters, stationery and so on.
- Some important new ingredient must be introduced to mark the change. This could be, for example, an increase in the top award, a new award for customer service, or a new award of the month.
- It must receive targeted and co-ordinated publicity by way of a special message from the Chief Executive, features in house magazines, one-off competitions for new posters, etc.

In summary, the re-launch needs to be treated just as seriously as the original launch itself. It represents a major opportunity for innovative thinking – from the professional marketers, the scheme managers and, above all, the customers of the scheme. The importance of planning and timing must not be overlooked.

Conclusion

This chapter has set out the different ways to plan the marketing strategy for the launch of the scheme, and having started a scheme, the ideas may be encouraged and the successes demonstrated both inside and outside the organisation. The chapter has also given specific examples for the scheme to be kept constantly in everyone's mind. It sets out when and how the scheme should be re-launched. Motivating employees is an important aspect of management today, and having a successful suggestion scheme is one of the best way of achieving this. All those who are involved with schemes are rewarded by the building of team spirit and the great knowledge that they are harnessing all the available talent within their organisation.

CHAPTER 7

EFFECTIVE ADMINISTRATION

Alexander Pope once said, "For forms of government let fools contest, whate'er is best administered, is best!"

But just what do we mean by administration? The word usually conjures up everything that can be wrong with systems. So why entitle a chapter in this way? Basically a degree of administration is essential to the success of the operation, but it must not be allowed to dictate to it. In considering administration, we shall explain the different approaches to use depending on the way the gathering and evaluation of ideas is structured, and determine how a manual or a computerised system could operate and the advantages of each. Throughout, we shall demonstrate how the team can function effectively.

The suggestions team

The differing roles that the suggestions team need to perform must be understood because this affects the whole operation. The team has to receive, register, arrange evaluation for and reply to all suggestions. It is the focal point for ideas throughout the workplace and must arrange for the distribution of publicity and suggestions forms. Team members should be available to talk to suggestors to help them express their ideas and crystallize their thoughts. The team will arrange for the presentation of awards and the provision of the gifts and cash for suggestors.

The team also needs to think of new ideas and publicity launches. In many organisations the marketing of the scheme will be performed in the same office; this subject was considered in Chapter 6.

Throughout, it must be remembered that every organisation is different, and the team that is eventually put in place must reflect its culture, just as every workforce is geared to a product or service. The culture of the organisation refers to the way different parts of it react with each other and how much of this is based upon tradition. This must be borne in mind if the system is to get off to the right start.

Team members

In its broadest sense the suggestions team will include many people. In large organisations it could comprise three or four administrators, a dozen committee members, and two or three hundred evaluators. The operation of the system works best if all these people see themselves as part of the 'team'.

However, this chapter will focus on the individuals at the centre who deal with every idea. How this core team is formed and selected can significantly affect the long term success of the system, so it is well worth spending time getting this right.

It is important that the Scheme Manager has an enthusiasm for suggestion schemes and has demonstrated a management flair for being positive to the receipt of new ideas. The most important assets any member of the team must possess are enthusiasm and positive thinking.

Different ways of assessing ideas are dealt with in Chapter 8, but these options will be alluded to here since they relate to the size and structure of the team needed to support them.

The work of the team

Ideally the responsibility for administration needs to be a full-time occupation. It is more effective to have two full-time administrators than to have six who must fulfil other responsibilities within the organisation. We have seen several schemes fail because the administrators were pulled in too many directions. If the suggestion scheme operates on a committee basis, then clearly the Chairperson may well only occupy that position for one day a month and at other times may be a functional director. (In this case he/she would be supported by an administrative office or secretariat.) However, if a Scheme Manager is appointed to spearhead the whole concept of ideas through the organisation, then he/she and the team should be a dedicated unit in the organisation's structure.

In small organisations there may seem to be insufficient ideas to justify a full-time team, but consideration should be given to having one full-time person who performs the masterminding of the scheme and couples this with some or all of the clerical duties. When the system takes off, then it will be easy to take on a part-time assistant and then a full-time one. The credibility a full-time team gives to the system is itself valuable in convincing both managers and employees that the organisation views suggestions seriously.

Where to place the team

There is no doubt that the higher up the team reports in the organisation the greater the credibility the system will have. There can, however, be many different places that the team may report.

Status

If a committee structure exists and the Chairperson reports directly to the Managing Director, then the team will be given considerable status. The Scheme Manager could also report to the Chief Executive or Managing Director, thus making the position more independent. If there is no committee structure, then it is important to have the Scheme Manager report to someone with status.

Personnel

Suggestion schemes and their teams are found most frequently in Personnel, no doubt because Personnel often handles many staff facilities. In several organisations, Personnel merely provides a service to line-managers whilst in others they retain a more traditional and powerful role. In some organisations Personnel is often seen by employees as playing a negative role. If the workforce views Personnel suspiciously, it may be counter-productive to place the team under that umbrella. It may be better to follow the example of organisations who have placed the team in the Financial Services area, since it is frequently called upon to put a value to adopted ideas. As an alternative to this, consider the Management Services or Internal Consultancy functions. Both of these are likely to take a macro-view of the organisation, which is important.

Secretariat

A final option to consider is what we shall call the secretariat. A secretariat often exists in major organisations to bring together issues affecting the whole of a multi-functional organisation. If it has credibility, then it may be another place to consider as its personnel should have an exceptionally good knowledge of the whole organisation, especially on corporate issues and current ideas coming forward from managers.

Size

We have often been asked "how many ideas can somebody deal with" or "how many people shall we need to handle a thousand ideas a year?" We can only provide guidelines. However, both the structure and the method by which the work is performed can vary considerably the number of personnel needed.

The Scheme Manager will need to perform tasks in the following areas:

- ideas for marketing the scheme
- compilation and provision of statistical information
- production of reports
- publicity of the scheme
- evaluation of ideas
- liaison with managers
- liaison with evaluators
- discussions with suggestors.

Other team members may be responsible for registering ideas and acknowledging them to suggestors; making contact with evaluators; replying to suggestors; compiling statistics; arranging rewards and attending promotional events.

The time spent on these activities can vary considerably over a space of time. However, two main factors affect the size of operation:

- how many ideas are received — this itself depends on the size of the workforce
- the method employed — the major difference being manual or computerised.

A manual or computerised system

If an organisation has less than 1,000 employees it is likely that even with full participation, i.e. everybody sending an idea a year, it can function without the aid of a computerised system. However, if there are more than 1,000 ideas a year, a computerised system becomes not only helpful but more essential. To try to run a manual system with more than 2,000 ideas a year will seriously affect its efficiency. Think how long it will take to check for a duplicate if one has to thumb through a list of titles. However, to not eliminate duplications may annoy evaluators and risk losing their goodwill.

The table on page 57 illustrates how the process may operate using each method.

Registering ideas

The success of the scheme depends on quick responses to suggestions. The full evaluation of ideas may lie outside the responsibility of the administrative

OPERATION	MANUAL SYSTEM	COMPUTERISED SYSTEM
Register idea	• write title in book • add details to suggestor's record card • allocate number or reference	• key into system • key into system • automatic allocation
Check for duplicate	• look through book	• automatic check (using key words)
Allocate to evaluator	• write in book	• key into system
Acknowledgement letter to suggestor	• type/write letter	• automatic generation
Monitor length of time with evaluator	• look through record book	• access records
Register reply	• write in book • delete from evaluator's outstanding list	• key into system and automatic deletion from outstanding list
Reply to suggestor	• type/write reply	• degree of autogeneration with keyed in sections
Filing	• cabinets to fill	• some hard copy to file, but much information in system
Management information eg.		
Ideas per suggestor	• count records	• automatic generation
Ideas on particular subject	• count records after reading through all	• automatic generation
Response time	• count replies and their time of evaluation then add the multiplied days and divide	• automatic generation

team, yet the initial acknowledgment is something that it can generate directly. A specific time target should be set to ensure that all ideas are acknowledged quickly. Ideally, all suggestors should be sent an acknowledgement on the day of receipt. A personal letter ought to be sent to the suggestor. If the team does not have the facility to do that then a hand-completed standard letter is better than a tear-off slip. Any sign of a personal interest in the individual is very important.

The suggestions team may also receive ideas verbally from employees visiting the office or phoning-in their idea. A pad of submission forms, therefore, should be handy to ensure that all the information needed is asked of the suggestor.

If ideas are received on the answerphone it is essential that the tape is changed when full. If it is not filled during a day, it still must be changed to ensure that there is no delay in processing the ideas. The idea must then be transcribed from the tape to a submission form. Again, tidiness is important, so set strict time targets. The idea is then processed in the same way as a written submission.

Once the idea has been acknowledged to the sender, it needs to be registered in some way. The amount of information that is registered at this stage will affect the information that can be recalled for the monitoring of scheme performance. It is useful to be able to record a large amount of information, because the statistics are an excellent way to obtain information on contribution and adoption rates and to compare the success of one area with another, i.e. how effective a particular advertising campaign has been; if particular grades of employeess are not making a contribution so they can be targeted for the future, etc.

Once registered and acknowledged, the ideas progress to the next stage. If sending new suggestors a memento for the submission of their idea the right time to do this is at the issue of the acknowledgement letter.

Checking for duplicates

The system must have a process to check for duplicates. This is essential for two major reasons. First, co-operation of evaluators will soon disappear if they find themselves having to reply to the same suggestion more than once. Whilst it is acceptable to go back to an evaluator and say that the idea has now been submitted three or four times and question whether it ought to be reconsidered, actually to send the idea could lead to a loss of support.

Second, by singling out an idea as a duplicate on receipt, it is possible to tell the suggestor immediately about the status of the previous idea on the subject. This is very important. If the original submission goes on to be adopted, an uninformed second suggestor will doubt the credibility of the scheme.

The actual method by which a check for duplicates is done will depend on the system devised. With a computerised system, the checking of duplicates can be a much more straightforward operation, either built in as an automatic or a request check.

Evaluation

Evaluation and who should be appointed as evaluators will be discussed in detail in the next chapter. However, it is appropriate to mention the team's connection with the administration of the evaluation process. The options for evalution are considerable. It is important, however, that the process be as streamlined as possible.

Full-time evaluators

The number of ideas being received determines whether independent, full-time evaluators can be appointed. This is the best system as there will be no conflict of priorities on their time between assessing the idea and undertaking other duties. If evaluators of this nature are appointed, then the relationship with the administrative unit will be forged at the inception and a good system will be devised to ensure that ideas are received by the evaluators quickly.

Part-time evaluators

If there are no full-time evaluators, then it is important that those people who have been appointed to evaluate ideas, receive them quickly and respond as soon as they can. A proper line of communication needs to be drawn up at the outset to ensure this works. If an organisation is relatively small, the contact with the evaluators may be on a personal basis. Several systems are in operation where a team member tours the building and discusses the ideas at first hand. If the operation is multi-site or very large, this is unlikely to be the most effective way of reaching the evaluators.

Communication

There are two methods of communicating ideas to evaluators. The first option is for a team member to telephone the evaluators and discuss the idea with them or visit them in a single-site operation. This will eliminate a large number of ideas having to be sent in writing. An expert should be able to evaluate many simple ideas on the telephone. Other ideas will need a deeper study, but this initial contact will prepare the evaluator for receipt of the idea.

There will be many times that a copy of the idea is needed by the evaluator. Therefore, a recognised system should be drawn up for carrying out this task quickly and efficiently. Fax or electronic mail should be considered, which some organisations use most effectively. On most occasions, a copy of the idea is sent. But if an organisation is reasonably small and there are few internal postal losses, it is quite acceptable to have the original circulate between the team and the evaluators. If a copy is sent, then the system devised must ensure that all correspondence bears the reference of the suggestion in order to guarantee that there is no misunderstanding about which suggestion is being assessed.

Under the second option, which we do not favour, a copy is sent to a department without prior telephone or personal contact. The idea is filed by the team until a reply is received from the evaluator. Although we have heard of organisations which say this does work, the method has defects:

- Sending ideas to the wrong evaluator. This can lose credibility for the scheme if it happens on more than a few occasions. It does not allow the evaluator to correct the mistake until days after the idea has entered the system.
- Ideas lost in post. This can lead to delays because the evaluator is not expecting the idea. Any postal losses in the internal system will not be detected until a follow-up request is sent.
- Low priority for idea evaluation. The evaluation form will take its place with that day's correspondence and may be seen as a low priority on the day. The idea might be put to one side and not examined.
- Repeat ideas and ones which the department know of. If several ideas are received on the same subject or on a subject which is being worked on at that time, the evaluator may become frustrated by the receipt of ideas and as a result his/her overall attitude towards the scheme may be affected.

Replying and rewarding

After the evaluator has responded to the team, they should have sufficient knowledge to reply to the suggestor. The reply should never refer to "rejecting", or "declining" the idea. It is far better to say why it cannot be adopted.

Awards and how to calculate the amount is covered in Chapter 8, but it is important to make sure that provision is made within the team for arranging to draw cash or cheques to pay awards; to distribute any gift that is given at an award ceremony; and to arrange for the provision of any certificate to be given to successful suggestors. How this is performed will depend very much upon the nature of an organisation.

Letters which can be generated from some form of word processor enable replies to be made on a personal basis. However, it is essential that this letter does not make the reason for non-adoption fit into a predefined space. Avoid at all costs the standard printed form that gives options which can be deleted. This may be quick and easy for administrators, but it is hardly conducive to making employees feel that their ideas are welcomed and being given serious thought.

Interim awards

One other aspect of rewards is the payment of interim awards. The administration of this process should be similar to the awards already mentioned. It is essential that there is a process to account for the size of the interim award so that when the final award is made, it is clear that the taxation rules are being complied with.

Statistics for management information

The final task that the suggestion scheme team will need to do is compiling statistics. It is essential at the outset to determine from managers what information they need. Overall success of the system will need to be measured. We have covered elsewhere the various information that should be provided. Suffice to mention here the need to consider the generation of this information within the administrative workload.

How the statistics are produced will depend upon the system's method of operation. These are easily obtained if the operation is computerised. If a computerised system is to be developed then the initial programming will need to make provision for accessing this information.

Filing and coding

An important aspect of any suggestion scheme office is its filing system. Even if the system adopted is completely open, each suggestion should be given a unique number. This number will then stay with the suggestion whenever it is referred to.

The allocation of a number with an alphabetical reference system can also aid the gathering of statistical information. For example, compare a system which progressively numbers each suggestion with one that uses individual segments of information. What does 13782 tell you? The answer is — very little. An alternative number could be 88/1342/E/WV. At a glance this tells you that the idea was submitted in 1988; that it was the 1,342nd idea that year; that it was submitted to the plant known as E (say Exeter); that the idea was submitted on a leaflet handed out at a Wednesday briefing Group (W); and that the idea related to valve improvements (V). The combinations are endless, but the example illustrates how simple the system is to operate.

It may be that this depth of information is not needed, but it will allow for any growth or development in the collection of data. Both manual and computerised systems will benefit from such an approach.

However at its simplest, suggestions need placing in numerical order in two separate files; those which have been evaluated and those which have not. It may be possible to keep all suggestions together when a small number are handled, but as the number increases, it will be essential that a separate file is allocated.

However, this split will soon prove insufficient if there are a large number to handle or if a telephone evaluation sifting process is in operation. In the case of the latter at least one extra file is needed in which to place ideas prior to telephone contact being made. Progressive number filing will not be suitable as it will be necessary to keep together all the ideas for a specific evaluator.

If appeals are allowed against decisions — this is essential to the credibility of the scheme — then consideration needs to be given to the processing of these. It is essential that these are kept separately and dealt with specially. Therefore, provision will need to be made for separate filing of ideas pending review.

Once it has been decided that the idea is to receive an award, it will take time to obtain a cheque and any certificate that is to be awarded. With this in mind it is important to again keep these ideas in a separate location within the filing system, although here they may be kept in numerical order.

Appeals

The administrative process must provide for handling appeals. If computerised the file must be capable of re-opening without detrimental consequences for the management.

Administratively otherwise, the appeal may then be dealt with as a normal suggestion.

Summary

The aspects that need to be provided for in the administrative team are to:

- receive idea
- register idea
- acknowledge idea
- distribute any initial gift
- arrange evaluation
- receive evaluation
- prepare papers for committee discussion
- distribute papers for committee meeting
- minute proceedings at committee meeting
- prepare letter to suggestor
- arrange award cheque/gift/certificate
- process papers internally-filing
- process any appeals
- distribute publicity literature
- produce management information.

It is all too easy to under-resource the administrative function. But this risks leaving willing evaluators waiting for ideas and eager suggestors with ill thought-out replies. Remember that quality is important and suggestors will be critical of replies that do not grasp the circumstances in which the suggestion was made. Ensure the team is properly trained in the organisation's business. The most important message of this chapter is that success of the whole system will revolve around the quality of the team. A quality team brings a quality scheme.

CHAPTER 8

ASSESSING AND REWARDING GOOD IDEAS

Good schemes ensure that ideas are assessed fairly and quickly and that the rewards are fair. It is important to distinguish between the evaluation of the idea (ie. what are the benefits of the organisation?) and determination of the award for the idea (ie. what is the appropriate award for the suggestor?). These are separate processes which involve different considerations. Organisations should separate them to avoid the obvious risks where a manager evaluates *and* rewards.

Evaluations

As we have said already it is essential that all ideas be viewed positively. How evaluations are performed is a specialist subject in its own right, and there are as many different methods as there are schemes. The method chosen will depend upon the size of the organisation and the required scope of the evaluations.

Below are listed options based upon the evaluators' link to the central suggestion scheme team. Whichever method is chosen, the evaluators must have some degree of training and have guidelines to assist them. Evaluators must take a positive approach to the idea, asking themselves, "How can I use this idea, even by adapting it". No evaluator should take the attitude, "How can I turn this down".

It is possible to combine aspects from the possibilities listed on page 65 which only show evaluation (not award or determination).

Manager of department

In this method each manager evaluates ideas relating to their span of control. If the organisation has several managers with similar areas of responsibility

METHOD	WHERE SUITABLE	ADVANTAGES	DIS-ADVANTAGES
Manager of Department*	• small companies • areas where there are not many ideas in large organisations	• no additional cost • expert in subject	• may cover up own shortcomings • may feel threatened and not have an open mind • tunnel vision may still prevail
Committee Evaluation	• where committee members have detailed knowledge	• seen to be fairer approach • reasons for not adopting ideas can be questioned by other members immediately	• expert may give quick answer to avoid appearing not to know • individual managers may feel on trial
Specialist Evaluator*	• large organisations where a considerable number of ideas are presented on an aspect of the company's operation	• unbiased evaluation	• costly to have full-time member of staff • managers may feel threatened

*may still come before a committee.

then the idea can be evaluated by the manager at the location of the suggestor and by another manager elsewhere. This increases the chance of a fair and unbiased evaluation. If a committee structure is involved, they all, or a selection of them, may make up the committee. However, if other managers are involved in the evaluation, the manager who is accountable must be the final arbitrator on adoption. This is important to ensure that managers who must implement the ideas do not feel that their control has been usurped.

The manager should not be the determinant of any award.

Specialist evaluator

This process has much to commend it. This method involves the appointment of a team (or individual) to evaluate ideas. These people will have no other priorities. This system must be properly resourced and have the facilities and the budget to carry out tests on ideas. Whilst the independent evaluator may determine the practicality of the idea, the final decision must involve the accountable manager, who makes the decision to adopt or not.

Committee evaluation

This method evaluates all ideas by committee. It may also use the same or a separate committee to determine the size of the award. It requires committee members to have a detailed knowledge of the ideas they are to evaluate. The administrator can bring all ideas before a meeting without prior circulation or can distribute the ideas to members first.

The former method is not very effective and will frequently delay ideas as specialist knowledge is not available without, for example, detailed drawings being examined.

In the second method, each department has a contact member in the committee. These are the link people to the administrative unit. With this method, the idea is sent to the link person who arranges evaluation within the department and then reports back at the next committee meeting, thus giving a more effective clearance.

Many places utilise committees successfully. Before deciding on this option, however, it is important to consider the reason for its existence.

ADVANTAGES OF A COMMITTEE

- Is seen to be fair.
- Gives opportunity for the members from other parts of the organisation to contribute and put in a different view.
- Can speed the evaluation of ideas involving several departments.

ADVANTAGES WITHOUT COMMITTEES

- Can avoid lengthy debate on minor issues.
- Will be cheaper to operate.
- Is much quicker as monthly committee meetings cause delay. Absence of members can add to this considerably.

If it is decided to introduce a committee, the next decision to make is to decide upon its composition. More and more organisations are deciding to have trade union representatives as members of the committee which gives credibility to a scheme. This extra involvement is an asset to most committees, whether it be done through official Trade Union channels or by having committee representatives selected by the workforce.

In small organisations it may be possible to include all accountable managers, or invite them to participate when ideas in their department are considered. In larger organisations, this may not be possible, therefore it is vital that the accountable manager agrees to adopt the idea.

It is important that a harmonious relationship exists between committee and line managers. We would advocate that the acceptability of an idea is the relevant manager's role, the committee challenging and questioning apparant illogicalities or defensiveness. Schemes which operate on the basis of the evaluation role undertaken solely by committee are likely to find a hostile line management resentful of the scheme which challenges their accountability.

Whichever of the above options is adopted, the administrative method by which ideas are sent to evaluators needs careful consideration.

Allowing for time

Evaluators should be set targets on the time they take to evaluate an idea. If this time is exceeded, they should send a progress report giving an approximate date when they expect to finalise their evaluation.

Evaluators have various courses open to them when assessing an idea. Following receipt of the idea they may be able to respond immediately. However, it is more likely that they will need to examine it or discuss it with another manager. Also, the evaluator could discuss the idea with the suggestor if the scheme reveals suggestors' names.

It is difficult to be precise on setting time targets because the evaluation can vary according to the subject of the idea and the structure of the organisation. It may be sensible to set different targets by subject matter and/or by level of manager.

In some large organisations ideas in a particular area may be considerable. If all are sent to a headquarters-level of management for evaluation, then there may be added delay and frustration caused by impractical ideas being submitted. For example, if a form is issued in an HQ department ask a few branch managers if the idea is practical first before asking the HQ manager.

Determination of awards

Once evaluation has taken place, an idea that is adopted is given an award. Regardless of the method of evaluation referred to above, the method of assessing the award is a separate process.

These two must be kept separate in order to avoid a conflict of issue. It would be wrong to be both arbiter and awarder. Thus having obtained the agreement of the responsible manager that the idea will be adopted, and the benefits provided by the evaluator, the award is calculated by a separate individual or a separate 'awards committee'. Both should be seen as independent.

In situations where the evaluator is the line manager, the independent body making the awards guarantees that the true value of the idea is awarded.

This may be performed in different ways:

Manager of Department/Specialist

We would not recommend that the original evaluator also determines the award and whilst another manager may take an unbiased view we feel it may not be seen by suggestors as a fair method.

Suggestion team

The Scheme Manager and his or her team should be detached enough from the evaluation to be able to determine awards. Advantages of using the team are that they will give a consistant approach which should be unbiased.

Additionally, awards can be determined without delay. Suggestors may however question the fairness of such a system.

Committee

Providing the determination of the award is kept as a separate role for the committee, or better still the only role for the awarding committee, this method will be viewed by suggestors as the fairest, especially if employee representatives play an active part. The disadvantage of a committee is that it can be a bottleneck which can cause delay.

Interim award

The establishment of an interim award can considerably aid in retaining the scheme's credibility. Interim awards tell the suggestor that evaluation will take some time, but that the initial impression of the suggestion is good and that it might be adopted.

There is no need for interim awards if suggestions will always be evaluated quickly. However, many complex engineering ideas need testing, and results may take several months. In these cases the payment of an interim award retains goodwill.

It is unwise to exceed the tax free amount for interest awards when paying an interim award or complications may arise if the idea is not adopted. However, if the interim award is being paid because the amount of benefit created by the suggestion's adoption is being calculated (and adoption is not in doubt) then a larger award should be paid.

Awards for adoption

If an idea is adopted, an award should always be paid. The basis on which this is done may determine the future success of the scheme. The award should fairly reflect the benefit to the organisation. Most awards are paid as a proportion of the benefit to the organisation and range from 10 to 50%. To pay less than 10% does not make for a fair scheme. A figure of 20% is the generally accepted amount. If too small a reward is paid, the suggestors within the organisation may feel that they are being treated unfairly. This could dissuade some people from submitting ideas. (Note the Inland Revenue concession on the payment of awards.)

Awards for direct benefits

To assess the amount of savings or benefit on which to base the award, it is normal practice to deduct any development or investment cost. With an idea that concerns a "one off" saving, the set-up cost is deducted from the savings. The resultant amount is used as the basis for the award. If the idea has savings that run over a number of years, then the savings may be calculated over the period of time concerned or five years, whichever is smaller. Deduct the development cost from the total savings, then divide by the number of years. The resulting net annual benefit is the one on which the award be based.

For example:

Development/Set-up costs	£100,000
Annual Savings	£80,000
Lifespan of Project	10 years

Savings over 5 years (£80,000 × 5)	£400,000
Development/Set-up costs	£100,000
Benefit after 5 years	£300,000
Net annual benefit	£60,000
Award at 20%	£12,000

This method provides a fair basis for both the organisation and the suggestor. There are other approaches. Many organisations pay a greater percentage for ideas which bring benefits over several years. For example, 10 per cent for one-off savings, 20 per cent for ongoing. It is very difficult to assess savings for years ahead and another alternative would be to pay a percentage (say 5 per cent) of actual savings for the next four years.

Awards for indirect benefits

Awards where a clear financial saving has been made or benefit created are not too difficult to assess. The problem arises where the benefits are not financial. There are, however, many different ways that these can be assessed. In some organisations, ideas are measured against specific criteria: ingenuity, ease of adoption, simplicity, extent to which this is a problem, etc. On this basis ideas can be placed in a bracket for an award.

This system can work well if all awards are generally small. But if the organisation pays out awards of several thousand pounds for ideas which save money, then the points system for other types of ideas must reflect this in its scale. An alternative is to award special prizes for ideas which fall into these difficult categories.

An example of the points system in a typical idea relating to customer service improvements could be as follows.

CRITERIA	**SCORE**
Original thought	5 out of 10
Benefit to the Customer	18 out of 20
Extra business potential	10 out of 20
Quality improvement	10 out of 20
Ease of implementation	16 out of 20
Cost of implementation	4 out of 10
Total	63 out of 100

AWARD SCALE FOR ADOPTED IDEAS

0 – 20 Points	£10
21 – 40 Points	£25
41 – 60 Points	£50
61 – 80 Points	£100
81 – 90 Points	£250
91 – 100 Points	£500

This is only a guide, and for ideas relating to other aspects of the business different criteria may be used.

With ideas that relate to safety issues, this same process may be used. However, it is possible to assess the probability of an accident occurring and its financial consequences and then reassess the changes in probability following adoption of the idea, thus giving a monetary position on which the award may be based. However, the objective must always be to ensure fair awards are paid.

Interest awards

Interest awards are called alternatively encouragement, incentive or merit awards. These terms adequately express the philosophy behind making the payment. The awards are made to encourage suggestors to try again; to reward a well thought-out idea which it will not be possible to implement; and to target areas in which staff have been reluctant to take part. A generous number of interest awards when a scheme is launched can help it to gain prestige. If at this or other time it is decided to have free draws as a boost, then the total award may not exceed £25 without the payment of tax unless the idea is adopted.

How much to award for encouragement is a matter of judgement, but an option is for evaluators to grade each idea. This can be incorporated into the determination of awards process.

It may be that interest awards are made by way of gifts instead of cash. This is perfectly acceptable, but care must be taken to ensure that staff do not feel that they are being treated unfairly. A catalogue of gifts to choose from can offer an exciting option.

Limit on awards

Many otherwise good and well-intentioned schemes have suffered because they have placed an artificial ceiling on awards. This is particularly true when the organisation has the potential for generating ideas that will make enormous savings. It is vital that goodwill is not lost by the adverse criticism that one poorly rewarded idea brings. If a suggestor develops an idea which brings a benefit of £2m per annum and receives a maximum of £200, then it would rebound on the organisation that made the award. Thus it is important that this aspect is considered when the scheme is introduced.

Several organisations use the artificial ceiling established by Inland Revenue guidelines, which fixes the tax-free limit at £5,000, but there is no need to do this.

Special competitions and awards

A good incentive to attract ideas on special subjects is to award prizes in specific areas. Thus, if an organisation were looking for good energy saving ideas, the best received each month could be awarded a prize of a relevant item, e.g. a microwave oven. An alternative is to have an extra award for every idea on that topic adopted or even a token prize for every idea sent in on the subject.

Suggestion of the Year awards

If extra awareness of the scheme is needed, then a Suggestor or Suggestion of the Year award should be introduced. This idea receives an extra award, which can be coupled with a special ceremony. The size of the award will depend upon the organisation. It need not be of significant size since the respect and recognition given by colleagues and family is of unique value for many workers.

The success of the venture may to some extent depend upon a special ceremony attached to the presentation. Some organisations run a whole-day event. The suggestors are taken out of the work environment and enjoy extra events not normally connected with the scheme, for example a river trip or helicopter flight. This could be followed by a lunch, then the ideas could be outlined to the judges by the suggestors. All this excitement adds to the day and makes it most enjoyable. The suggestors will talk about this and generate considerable interest.

Multiple suggestors

Ideas may be submitted by a group of staff.This should be encouraged. In fact, this can aid the suggestion since it is discussed in a group before submission. Apart from being aware that the taxation rules apply per suggestion, not per suggestor, there should not be any difference in the way the idea is processed.

If the suggestion is submitted with one lead name while declaring other peoples' interests, then replies should be sent to that name. Otherwise a reply would go to every suggestor. If an award is paid, it is much better to award each suggestor a separate cheque than have one between the group.

Appeals

When designing the scheme, consideration must be given to appeals. If the scheme is to be seen as fair, then appeals must be allowed to take place. These appeals should be accepted on two grounds. The first is when the suggestor feels that the idea has been misunderstood or that new or alternative facts have come to light. This will entail the relatively simple task of returning to the original evaluator, passing on the additional information and arranging for a re-evaluation. These ideas should be kept separately in the system. If committee adjudication is involved, then it will be essential to ensure that the members are aware of the full facts.

The second type of appeal is when a suggestor feels that the idea has been adopted some time after the idea was turned down. This can occur for a variety of reasons. The most common is a changed economic situation or the more specific change in personnel in the organisation. This can be particularly true of ideas involving marketing or pricing. If appeals are not allowed, then the result can be loss of credibility and the creation of an unfair feeling about the scheme. Therefore the message is clear: always allow appeals to take place. We do recommend that a time limit be placed upon appeals, and experience has shown that three years after original submission is a reasonable cut off time.

A decision will need to be made about the mechanics of processing appeals. Clearly, provision must be made to deal with these separately and quickly. Some organisations ensure that appeals are looked into by a different evaluator. But the size of the organisation and the limitations of sufficient experts in the subject area of the suggestion must be considered. Appeals should be referred to a high level in the organisation. Appeals must, however, be seen to be fair. It is important that the rules of the scheme clearly set out the method by which appeals can be made.

Summary

This section has dealt with the many methods of evaluating and rewarding ideas. Whatever methods are chosen, the scheme should always aim for:

- fairness in evaluation
- fairness in rewards
- speed of replies.

If an organisation can get these three things right, not only will it have a recipe for success, but it will also find publicising the scheme easy.

SECTION III

CASE STUDIES

SUGGESTION SCHEME

SUGGESTION SCHEME

History

The Rover Group first launched the suggestion scheme in 1973 to combine the former BMC and Pressed Steel Fisher Schemes.

The present Rover Group Suggestion Scheme has developed from this as a way of encouraging employees to have a real sense of involvement in the business. The Suggestion Scheme is an opportunity for our people to influence directly the success of the business, and their growing involvement is very encouraging.

Organisation

Managing Director

Personnel Director

Personnel Operations Director

Employee Relations Director

Suggestion Scheme Manager

Eleven Site Suggestion Scheme Committees

Policy

Policy governing the operation of the Suggestion Scheme is determined by Rover Group Personnel Staff.

Responsibility

A suggestion scheme manager is the person responsible for planning and controlling the Scheme within Rover Group, ensuring consistency in interpreting the rules, applying procedures and making awards.

Operation of Scheme

The Scheme is operated through Suggestion Scheme Committees. There must be five elements to form a quorum.

- Director or Executive to act as chair (plus casting vote)
- Company Suggestion Scheme Manager to co-ordinate and ensure consistency
- Managers from major departments, e.g. Conformance Engineering, Personnel, Production, Commercial, Product Engineering and Finance
- Local Suggestion Scheme Officers
- Representatives of Trade Unions

Committee Functions

- To approve decisions on adoptability of suggestions
- To adjudicate on queries of eligibility, acceptability and appeals
- To unblock where progress is reported to be impeded
- To make award decisions

Suggestion Scheme Officer

The person responsible for administering the scheme locally.

Marketing

As part of the drive to increase the level of participation by employees, the Scheme is supported by regular advertising and incentive campaigns.

For example, details of award winners are displayed on posters throughout all the sites with the information repeated in employee bulletins and transmitted on each site's electronic noticeboard system.

Local activity is supported by centrally generated campaigns, e.g. "the best green issue" suggestion during a given period wins an environmentally friendly "Green Mini".

The items of TV commercials are adopted for use on posters to provide a link between employees and the market theme.

A key part of the strategy to encourage participation is to ensure the rapid processing of suggestions and subsequent implementation. The company's management network system is geared to this objective.

Basis of awards

Our maximum award is £5,000, plus an attractive motor car for suggestions that save £150,000. For a suggestion that saves £100,000 the award is £5,000 plus a colour television. Awards are based on 20% of the net savings calculated over 12 months. When the benefits cannot be calculated, special awards are made and these range from £15 to £2,000 depending on merit. Interest awards are also paid as an encouragement and these are usually up to £25.

Success stories

Participation in the Rover Group Suggestion Scheme has risen in five years from 6% to 40% currently and increasing. Awards to employees have risen from £75,000 to £500,000 and saving to the company from £500,000 to £3.5 million.

UK Statistics for 1988

Number of employees	40,000
Eligible employees	40,000
Ideas received	12,000
Participation rate	30%
Ideas adopted	1,900
Success rate	16%
Total savings	£3.5 million
Highest award	£5,000 plus car (Maestro)
Other awards	Flight on Concorde, helicopter ride, meal at hotel, TVs, video recorders, microwaves, cameras
Total awards	£500,000

IDEAS!

History

Over the past 10 years Coloroll has grown from a small company employing 450 people to a large home fashion group employing 10,000.

One of the most important problems of growth which had to be managed was the potential loss of the "family" atmosphere and the involvement of, and communication with, employees.

Fortunately the problem was nipped in the bud when two and a half years ago an intensive employee involvement programme was launched. This began with Team Briefing and was quickly followed by other initiatives of which the "Ideas!" scheme was considered one of the most important.

The objective of the scheme, therefore, is the involvement of employees, and for this reason we aim for a high participation rate. All ideas are treated seriously.

Organisation

At present, there are approximately 10,000 employees working for 15 different companies. The companies run autonomously and group involvement is limited to introduction of the scheme and thereafter introducing ideas, competitions, posters, etc to maintain enthusiasm for the scheme. Everything else is handled on site.

Each company, therefore, has its own Ideas! clerk who meticulously records ideas and distributes them anonymously to investigators (the most suitable manager). Once investigated the idea with its response is considered at the monthly committee meeting which is made up of a cross-section of employees, and chaired by a director. The committee has the power to award and to dispute an investigator's response.

At every stage a letter is sent to the idea originator to keep him or her informed of progress.

Marketing

The scheme is introduced to new companies at the Team Brief, and on the same day lively posters and bright yellow Ideas! boxes appear everywhere, all featuring our now famous Colorollie. The scheme is explained in more detail in an introductory leaflet, a copy of which is handed to every employee.

From the word go the scheme is seen as "fun" rather than "work", and of course it is seen as generous. This means that we get lots of ideas, and though many of them are not implemented they still receive an encouragement award because we are happy to pay for the interest and involvement displayed by *all* idea originators.

Awards

Every idea receives an encouragement award. The first idea receives an "I'm a Colorollie" mug making the originator a member of the Ideas! Club. After that there is a choice of collectable wine and beer glasses, all produced by Coloroll, and we're shortly adding key rings to the selection.

Successful cost-saving ideas receive 20% of the first year's saving less costs. Successful ideas for which there is no obvious cost-saving are granted awards as follows:

- of some merit — £10
- a good idea that will be implemented — £25
- an excellent idea that will be implemented — £50
- an outstanding idea that will be implemented — £250

Furthermore all ideas are considered for one of six Managing Directors' Idea of the Year award of £1,000, and for the Chair's Idea of the Year award of £5,000.

To encourage on-going participation, prizes are given from time to time. All ideas for a particular period are put into a draw and the prizes range from soft-toy Colorollie to a weekend in London. A more recent encouragement involves every participator receiving an extra award of a Coloroll car sticker. These are proving quite popular.

Success stories

Bearing in mind that our scheme was designed primarily to involve employees more in their company, our biggest success must be our participation rate of 55% on average to date, beating our target of 40%.

We are working to improve our implementation rate because we are off target of 17% with only 9% of ideas adopted in 1989. However, taking out those companies new to the scheme this improves to 11%. The generosity of our scheme has proved itself, too, for whilst over two years the scheme has cost us £36,000 in awards, we have realised over nine times that in savings, beating our target of a 1:8 ratio.

And what of our special ideas? Well, our current success is a "Singing Mug" idea which won the Customer Services section of the UKASS/Industrial Society Idea of the Year finals. The idea prolonged the life of the mugs singability (most of us would have preferred he never had the idea!).

We have had four ideas which have saved around £20,000 p.a. each, and all these in production areas where we are always endeavouring to keep our costs down.

The biggest saving to date of £70,000 p.a. enabled us to cut out the waste when matching up ready-made curtains and promises to pay the originator £14,000.

A non-cost-saving idea which has proved particularly good is a Coloroll Fun Fortnight, which is now an annual event that raises thousands of pounds for charity. Another idea suggested safety posters produced by Coloroll employees, creating a fun competition and eight effective, colourful posters.

UK Statistics

	1987/88	**1988/89**
Number of employees	5,000	6,000
Eligible employees	4,317	5,742
Ideas received	3,022	2,479
Participation rate	70%	43%
Ideas adopted	245	235
Success rate	8%	9%
Total savings	£136,199	£206,136
Highest award	£9,000	£14,000
Total awards	£16,787	£19,207

KINGSTON AND DUNSFOLD SUGGESTION SCHEME

History

The Kingston and Dunsfold sites are part of British Aerospace PLC and the home of the Harrier Aircraft. They have a large highly skilled workforce, a complex manufacturing process and a large home/export market.

The Suggestion Scheme programme is currently enjoying a successful period, 1988 being the best year of its nine year existence. This is due to a number of major changes and a reappraisal of where the scheme was going.

The Scheme was set up in 1979 with the aim of improving general efficiency and achieving cost savings. The approach was initially one of caution. With a reorganisation of the business in the late Eighties came a commitment from senior management to recognise the benefit that can be achieved from Suggestion Schemes. From then on the scheme moved from success to success.

Organisation

The Scheme is open to all employees: this is necessary to satisfy Inland Revenue regulations. A suggestion must not be part of an employee's normal work or duties. Payment is calculated as 30% of the first year's savings less any non-recurring charges to a maximum of £2,000 per suggestion. These suggestions are assessed by a committee which meets on a monthly basis.

The committee is made up as follows: The Manager of Dunsfold site (Chair), Head of Resources Dept. Kingston, Resources Dept. Secretary (Secretary), a senior representative from Design, two representatives from Production Centre Management, the Head of Cost Reduction Dept., an Employee Communications Officer, three shop floor Union Representatives and a full-time Suggestion Scheme Co-ordinator. This gives a broad and balanced consideration of any suggestion discussed.

All suggestions are initially received by the Suggestion Scheme Co-ordinator who allocates them for investigation and assessment and immediately informs the suggestor of the receipt of suggestion; this is most important. The Co-ordinator usually investigates and assesses 60% of suggestions, the Cost Reduction Dept. 30% and the balance by experts from other departments.

The aim of the Suggestion Committee is to either make a final payment, an interim payment, usually £25-£50 (subject to more detailed investigation), or to reject the suggestion, all within two months of receipt. This occurs in 95% of cases.

Marketing

The success of the Scheme is due to a number of factors. These include a commitment from middle management, constant advertising by a number of methods — posters, internal and external publications, communication services, special awards, e.g. free trip to the U.S.A., plus the assistance of a full time Co-ordinator to regularly meet and discuss ideas with the suggestors on a one-to-one basis. One of the most important improvements to the scheme has been the increase in successful ideas. This has been encouraged by a change in layout of the Suggestion Scheme Form. A more positive approach is now required by the suggestor. The suggestor is requested to state the problem, then the solution. No longer do we receive bland statements such as "I suggest we use less electricity"; "We need more parking spaces"; "People should use the telephone less", etc.

With the increase in successful suggestions it has now become even more important to recognise suggestors' achievements. An award is now a high profile event. A presentation lunch, a photo call and prizes awarded by a Director are the order of the day.

Success stories

One point which has emerged in the last few years has been a hard core of two dozen suggestors who are constantly trying and succeeding with suggestions. Once someone has been successful we encourage him/her to try again - this approach works.

Among the top awards in 1988 were: one suggestor received £2,000; three received over £1,000; one suggestor won two tickets to the U.S.A. (the same suggestor reached the final of the UKASS/Industrial Society Suggestion of The Year competition) and a flood of innovative and money saving ideas.

One area that needs attention is the lack of suggestions coming from non-manufacturing areas. This may occur because of a broader definition of job description and a reticence to criticise established practices. Solutions to this problem are currently being discussed and ideas are being canvassed.

UK Statistics for 1988

Number of employees	5,051
Employees eligible	5,051
Ideas received	369
Participation rate	7.3%
Ideas adopted	122
Success rate	33%
Total savings	£71,092
Total awards	£11,541

LUCAS SUGGESTION SCHEME

History

The Lucas Suggestion Scheme was launched in 1921 and has now generated over three million suggestions and continues to play an important part in the constant drive to improve competitiveness in the Aerospace, Automotive and Industrial markets worldwide.

The Scheme has the support of the Chairman and Directors of Lucas Industries and also receives active operational support from local plant managers, employees and Trades Unions.

The Scheme is based on the simple belief that management does not have the monopoly of good ideas and that the individual employee is often best placed to identify the causes of local problems and to work out creative solutions. To succeed the Scheme must continuously motivate all employees to submit their ideas for improving efficiency and raising standards of performance and must acknowledge their contributions through a system of appropriate awards.

The objectives of the Scheme are:

- to provide a comprehensive and systematic process for employees to voluntarily communicate their ideas to management on how to improve the operation of the business
- to reward those employees whose suggestions are accepted and to encourage those whose ideas are the result of careful thought, even if not adopted
- to promote an atmosphere in which change is more readily accepted.

Organisation

The essential focus of the Suggestion Scheme is at plant level, where it is managed through a Plant Suggestion Scheme Committee consisting of management and employee representatives supported by a Suggestions Secretary. Currently there are 40 UK Lucas plants operating a Suggestion Scheme.

At group level, a senior manager co-ordinates all plant schemes and ensures they operate within a general policy framework.

Procedures are kept simple: employees ideas are submitted on suggestion forms which are freely accessible in all plants.

On receipt of the suggestion, the local suggestions secretary ensures the suggestion is registered and forwarded to the appropriate Departmental Manager for investigation and subsequent report.

Anonymity is preserved until final decisions have been made on the feasibility of the idea concerned.

Adopted suggestions are then submitted to the local plant suggestions committee whose job it is to assess the value of award. Each committee can make awards for adopted suggestions up to £750.

Good ideas that for one reason or another cannot be adopted are eligible for Merit Awards up to £25.

All suggestors receive personal reply letters following the investigation and assessment procedures.

Marketing

Although an efficient and just administration of a Scheme is probably the best insurance against failure, there can be no doubt of the importance of positive publicity in maintaining the interest and in improving the response of employees.

At the end of each year all adopted suggestions are reviewed again within each subsidiary company and the best are awarded an additional Director's Award of up to £1,000 each.

Outstanding suggestions considered to be deserving of £1,250 or more receive a Chairman's Award from the Chairman of Lucas Industries. These awards are presented at a special ceremony held in Birmingham. Husbands, wives or friends are invited to the presentation ceremony and later join the winning suggestors for lunch. The highest individual Chairman's Award to date has been £4,000.

A special poster publicising the results of the Annual Awards is circulated throughout the Lucas Plants. In addition our bi-monthly internal newspaper *Lucaslife* provides the Suggestion Scheme with good publicity throughout the year and serves to keep the Scheme foremost in the employees' minds. Experience has shown that employees reading of their colleagues' awards are motivated to submit ideas of their own. There is the added advantage that *Lucaslife* is conveyed into the employee's home.

At frequent intervals new posters advertising the Suggestion Scheme, in different forms, are circulated to all plants.

A Suggestion Scheme information pamphlet is made available to all employees.

Basis of awards

In calculating a particular award for an adopted suggestion, originality, ingenuity, careful thought, practical benefits and cost savings are all carefully considered by each plant suggestions committee.

A committee consists of a senior manager as chairman, an equal number of elected employees and nominated management representatives, e.g. 2+2 maximum, plus the local plant suggestions secretary.

In cases of intangible suggestions a points system is used to ensure consistency of approach and to determine an award. Points are awarded for importance of Change, Application and Originality.

Success stories

Industry Year 1986

Lucas Industries plc were awarded a Best Suggestion Scheme award in the Ideas Unlimited Competition sponsored by The Industrial Society/BBC TV.

1988 Top Suggestion

Bernard Jackson, a tool technician from Lucas Aerospace Defence Fabrications Burnley, received a 1988 Chairman's Award of £4,000 for an innovative CNC lathe jaw location for machining forward-closing rocket domes more efficiently, thus saving £186,000 per annum.

1988 Chairman's Awards

Roger Lane, a setter operator at Lucas Aerospace Engine Systems Birmingham, received £3,000 for designing and developing a vertical lapping machine attachment which improves the accuracy of final surface finishing to within millionths of an inch. Because of the ingenuity of the suggestion a patent application has been filed.

A Lucas suggestor has two awards

At our South Wales Braking Plant, commercial shaft brakes were packed nine to a crate prior to despatch to Volvo in Sweden. A suggestor from the packing department recommended that a further three shaft brakes could be packed in the same crate—increasing each pack to 12 shaft brakes. On investigation, and agreement with Volvo, this simple idea was adopted, and the suggestor received a 1986 Chairman's Award of £1,000.

Volvo senior management were very impressed with this idea, and to show appreciation invited the Lucas suggestor and his wife to visit Gothenberg in Sweden for three days as their guest. Volvo are noted for having an extremely good suggestion scheme operating throughout their plants in Sweden.

UK Statistics for 1988

Number of employees	35,000
Employees eligible	27,000
Ideas received	5,051
Participation rate	18%
Ideas adopted	2,352
Success rate	46%
Total savings tangible	£1.5 million
Highest award	£4,000
Total awards	£173,000

STAFF SUGGESTIONS SCHEME

History

The first scheme to encourage Inland Revenue staff to make suggestions was started in 1922. Successful suggestors were rewarded by a note to their reporting officer so that credit could be given on their annual report.

In 1948 the Inland Revenue started to award book tokens to successful suggestors. From 1965 all awards were made in cash and the number of suggestions began to grow. The growth reached its peak in the mid-1970s with the presentation of a then record award of £300 by the Chair of the Board of Inland Revenue.

Following a report by a joint management and trade union working party set up in 1983, the scheme was revamped into its present form.

Organisation

The Suggestions Committee is made up of nominees from management and the trade unions. The full Committee meets at least once a year, but the day-to-day work is done by various sub-committees. Most of the work is done by correspondence although some cases are discussed at quarterly meetings.

The Committee is supported by a secretariat of Chair (part-time), Deputy Chair, Secretary and three other staff.

Suggestions are sifted and registered by the secretariat and then passed to specialists for their opinion. The specialists categorise the suggestions as either adopted, not adopted, or acceptable in principle. They are asked to say whether there will be any financial benefit in adopting a suggestion and, if so, whether it will exceed £2,000 per annum. Details are then circulated between the management and trade union nominees for vetting. The Chair and Deputy Chair monitor for consistency between the sub-committees and they take part in the decision making process.

Marketing

In 1984 a publicity sub-committee was set up to market the scheme. The Inland Revenue's Publicity Unit was asked to produce two posters. The theme chosen was that big things grow from little beginnings. "Acorns From Which Big Oak Trees Grow" was selected as the first poster design and it was simultaneously adopted as the logo of the scheme. This logo appears on all stationery and communications and aims to give the scheme a recognisable identity.

There is a quarterly magazine called *Ideas* which reaches all staff and contains details of the Committee, award winners and topics currently under review. The Chair of the scheme has a regular column in the magazine about matters of current interest and information.

Forms, including the suggestion's submission form, have been redesigned to make them user friendly and of a high professional design quality. The Merit Notes awarded to suggestors have also been redesigned. These Notes are personally signed by the Chair of the suggestions scheme.

The sub-committee hope to produce a video to publicise the scheme further some time within the next 18 months. They will also be looking in the near future at whether gifts and other promotional aides have any place in the scheme.

Basis of awards

Adopted suggestions are put into one of the following categories:

CATEGORY A	**AWARD**
A suggestion considered to merit official recognition.	A Merit Note. An award of £10 or £30 may also be given.

Unquantified savings:

CATEGORY B	
A suggestion likely to result in a *minor* improvement in efficiency or effectiveness.	Merit Note plus an award of £50 or £100.
CATEGORY C	
A suggestion which brings about a *significant* improvement.	Merit Note plus an award of £200, £300, £400 or £500.

CATEGORY D A suggestion which gives rise to a *substantial* improvement.	Merit Note plus an award of over £500.

Quantifiable savings:

CATEGORY E	Merit Note plus up to 10% of the first year's savings up to £22,500 of savings; above £22,500 – fifteen times the square root of the savings.

A suggestion is acceptable in principle if it seems worth adopting but cannot be implemented for the time being, i.e. within twelve months. Such a suggestion earns a Merit Note and an award of up to £25. If it is implemented later, a further award may be made.

If a suggestion is not adopted, the suggestor may be commended for constructive thought, effort or presentation. A small award, up to £25, may also be made.

Success stories

Since the revamping of the scheme in 1983, participation has increased. In 1984 £4,000 was paid to a suggestor. In 1987 £9,000 and a weekend holiday for two was awarded for a suggestion about the banking of large tax payments received. In October 1988 £10,000 and a champagne flight on Concorde was awarded to a suggestor who put forward the idea of a more cost-effective way of dealing with a tax collection matter.

As well as setting new levels of record awards, more suggestors are getting higher awards. The average savings achieved by the scheme since 1983 are nearly £1.5 million per annum.

Average yearly statistics as of 31.3.89

Number of employees	66,500
Employees eligible	66,500
Ideas received	3,927
Participation rate	7%
Ideas adopted	269
Success rate	7%

Total savings	£906,842
Highest award	£10,000
Other awards	5 of over £1,000
Total awards paid	£48,000 last year

STAFF SUGGESTION SCHEME

History

It is thought that both the former Ministry of National Insurance and the former National Assistance Board (NAB) operated staff suggestion schemes from at least 1948. After amalgamation into the Ministry of Social Security in 1966, the schemes continued to operate with separate committees until 1982, when radical changes were made to the scheme.

Organisation

The present scheme is a centralised one covering the whole Department, and is controlled by the Efficiency Unit, which is part of the Central Resource Management Division reporting to the Principal Establishment Officer. The Efficiency Unit is also responsible for various monitoring activities and for maintaining a register of all Consultancy, Inspection and Review studies. Eleven staff work on the scheme in the Unit.

The Efficiency Unit sifts out duplicate and certain other suggestions before referring the rest to the appropriate evaluating branch, either by a file, meeting or telephone. The most promising suggestions are "fast streamed". There is a target period of three months for clearing suggestions, with four weeks for those which are fast-streamed. Advice from the evaluators is scrutinised by the Efficiency Unit and challenged where necessary. Progress is chased by eight-weekly reminder lists issued to the section heads of evaluating branches, with copies sent to senior managers.

The Grade 7 in the Efficiency Unit is the Chair of the Suggestions Committee, which generally makes the larger awards, having delegated to the Chair awards of up to £100. The Committee (12 members) is composed of representatives from evaluating branches and from DSS local offices. The Trades Union side have declined to be represented.

Until 1982, all suggestions were referred to one of several committees. There were also separate "policy" and major award committees. At about that time, however, the duties of the policy committee and the major awards committee (a central Civil Service committee) and the "scrutinising" responsibilities of the other committees were transferred to the Efficiency Unit. This left the present Departmental committee free to consider the larger awards.

The scheme is fully computerised, from initial checking for duplication of ideas and acknowledging the suggestions, through regular progress-chasing, to the final decision letters.

Marketing

There is firm top management support for the scheme, which is demonstrated through an annual presentation of the major awards by the Secretary of State or one of his/her Ministers and by the attendance of many senior officers. The main publicity for the scheme is achieved by regular circulars to all staff giving details of awards. The monthly house journal *Window* also regularly contains details of individual successes, as well as publicising the annual presentation.

Basis of awards

Where the benefits of an idea are quantifiable (about 15% of accepted ideas), awards are based on the Civil Service formula of 10% of the first year's savings (where they do not exceed £22,500) and 15 times the square root of any savings where they exceed £22,500. The basic award figure may then be adjusted by the Committee (usually downwards) to reflect features such as the proximity of the idea to the suggestor's duties, the duration of the savings and originality/effort.

Where the benefits are not quantifiable, a judgement is made - usually by the Chair but occasionally by the Committee. There are no non-cash awards at present.

Success stories

Quantified first-year savings in 1988/89 amounted to £6.25 million and awards paid totalled £148,500. The highest award for one idea is £19,500 (shared between six people); the first-year savings from which amounted to £3.5 m. The highest award for an individual is £15,000 for an idea which saved over £1.5 million a year.

The number of suggestions has been rising for some years. The rise in 1988/89 being 70%, from 8,200 to 14,000. In 1989/90, the number expected is 16,500.

Statistics for 1988/89

Number of employees	83,000
Employees eligible	83,000
Ideas received	14,131 (8,000 excluding duplicates)
Participation rate	17%
Ideas adopted	850
Success rate	10%
Total savings	£6.25 Million
Highest award	£19,500 (shared), £15,000 (individual)
Total awards	£148,500

Brainwaves

BRAINWAVES

History

British Airways launched Brainwaves in June 1983. A significant relaunch was undertaken in June 1986, which included an increase in the top award to £10,000. Further changes, including revisions to logo, promotional literature and organisational support, were introduced in May 1989.

The objective is to encourage British Airways staff to put forward original and imaginative ideas which will benefit British Airways and its stakeholders through improved efficiency, lower costs or greater revenue, improved safety and better customer, employee or community relations. Informally Brainwaves is also recognised as an excellent opportunity for staff development. Suggestors are encouraged to develop their ideas to the maximum extent before submitting them for assessment.

Organisation

Brainwaves is administered by a small team of two people reporting within the Airline's Internal Business Consultancy unit. They support a Central Awards Team which has specific responsibility for policy, confirmation of significant awards, and selection of Awards of the Month and Year.

Reporting to the Central Team are four departmental teams who consider suggestions in respect of engineering, technical, customer services, and central services respectively. Each departmental team is empowered to make payments of up to £250; larger awards require confirmation by the Central Team.

Teams meet monthly and membership comprises equal numbers of suitably qualified management and staff drawn from across the Airline. Participation is in addition to normal duties, and the success of the scheme is heavily dependent on the personal commitment of the individuals involved. The Chair of each Team is a management nominee.

Suggestions are assessed in the workplace by line management and supervisors appropriate to the particular suggestion.

Marketing

Brainwaves is promoted primarily as a scheme which produces financial benefits for the Airline, whether directly through lower costs and more revenue or indirectly as a result of better customer service, etc. As a matter of policy, it is not identified as a "morale booster". Recently, within the Airline's management community, the scheme has been presented as a legitimate tool in the drive to reduce costs.

Brainwaves is publicised through a variety of media ranging from posters to promotional videos. It is regularly featured in The Annual Report and Accounts and in in-house publications including interest features in British Airways News. All awards of £1,000 and above are presented personally by Sir Colin Marshall, Deputy Chairman and Chief Executive, which demonstrates commitment to the scheme at the most senior levels.

Specific promotions are now a feature of Brainwaves. They are generally of short duration, e.g. three months, and cover themes such as waste or the environment. Suggestions are eligible for special awards, usually non monetary, in addition to any normal Brainwaves award made.

In addition to individual awards for a suggestion Brainwaves offers monthly and annual awards. Of the two annual awards, both presented by the Chairman of British Airways, one is targeted specifically towards the best suggestion in the area of Customer Service, a decision designed to recognise the importance of such suggestions in a competitive service environment.

Basis of awards

Monetary awards are made based on both the merit of the suggestion and the assessed annual savings or revenue gain. Within a maximum limit of £10,000, awards of up to 15% of annual savings are made.

Awards of the Month and Year are determined by ingenuity and merit and not necessarily on the basis of strict financial benefit to the Airline. Although they may include a monetary element, gifts and travel related incentives are a feature of these awards and also those mentioned previously which arise from special promotions.

Success stories

Since the launch of Brainwaves in 1983 there have been many successful suggestions which have brought significant benefits to British Airways and its customers.

Working in a high technology area, aircraft engineers have been particularly successful in exploiting opportunities for new techniques and procedures which either increase efficiency or reduce costs. In one notable example, a sophisticated redesign of a warning switch dramatically reduced the incidence of in-flight turn backs on Concorde with consequent cost and customer service benefits. The suggestion, which was presented in meticulous detail, subsequently won the Award of the Year.

In 1986, a British Airways engineer won the first Industrial Society/BBC "Ideas Unlimited" trophy for the best individual suggestion in the UK. This success was followed in 1988 with the award for the best idea in the Technology category.

Elsewhere in the Airline, a recent suggestion which proposes a change to the way we hold and manipulate one of our fares computer databases has led to savings and additional revenue opportunities which are assessed to be worth in the region of £0.5 million.

Statistics for Financial Year 88/89

Number of employees	49,000 (Average)
Employees eligible	49,000 (Scheme shortly to be extended to include retired staff)
Ideas received	2,300
Participation rate	4.7%
Ideas adopted	500
Success rate	22%
Total savings	£850,000
Highest award	£10,000 (Scheme maximum)
Other awards	Range of gifts, including tickets to destination of choice
Total awards	£93,000

COLT IDEAS CLUB

History

Colt International had always had a suggestion scheme, but by 1985 it was moribund, producing very few suggestions despite increased awards. During that year we carried out a QED programme to motivate staff and generate ideas. This was so successful that it was decided to relaunch the suggestion scheme under the Colt Ideas Club banner with commitment from the top, far less restrictions and a simpler form of assessment. This has been consolidated and a new logo was launched for the Club in 1989 in line with the quality culture which the company now wishes to promote. It has always been important to Colt that the Ideas Club is closely identified with the company and its aims and objectives.

Organisation

The scheme is administered by a Co-ordinator on a part-time basis. All ideas are passed to the Director who is the functional head of the department to which the idea relates. Although not expected to assess each one personally, it is the Director's responsibility to see that they are returned by due dates with a comprehensive assessment. The ideas are then adjudicated by a Committee consisting of the Board of Directors, the Marketing Manager and the Co-ordinator. This facilitates implementation as the necessary authority is present.

Marketing of scheme

The original Ideas Club was promoted by means of posters and newsletters. The present scheme was launched after a questionnaire had been circulated to all personnel and the results analysed. A launch pack was sent to each employee containing a personalised letter, a rules and procedures booklet to help with the submission of ideas and a pen with a rotating barrel which shows various messages related to suggestions.

Each new employee attends an induction course and the Co-ordinator has a 40 minute slot to explain the Ideas Club. A case study is used to illustrate the principle of submitting an idea. New employees work in groups to submit ideas for improvement of a mythical company.

Basis of awards

There is a scale of awards as follows:

- £10 for a good idea which for one reason or another cannot be implemented.
- £30 for a good idea which will be implemented — these ideas do not normally demonstrate any significant saving but add to either the safety of employees, the quality of their environment or procedural changes.
- £75 for an excellent idea which will be implemented. These ideas have further-reaching effects and may well demonstrate savings which cannot be quantified.
- £200 for an outstanding idea. This is the upper limit for ideas where the savings cannot be quantified.
- £200+ for ideas with quantifiable savings. The savings are based on a percentage of the first year's savings assessed against agreed criteria such as ease of implementation, degree of innovation, degree of work involved by suggestor, etc.

Success stories

Colt has featured on the Ideas Unlimited programme on BBC TV and won the award for the Most Improved Suggestion Scheme. We have also been runners-up on the same programme for the Best Suggestion.

We have received ideas which have saved thousands of pounds by modification of machines or use of materials.

A guillotine operator suggested that by moving his templates around he could produce one more unit from a sheet of material than had previously proved possible. This produces considerable savings.

One of our turret press operators noticed that our existing method produced scratches on the material as it was moved round on the bed of the machine. He devised a brush using an existing sealing brush strip to sweep the material and eliminate the scratches.

UK Statistics for 1988

Number of employees	550
Employees eligible	542 (All except the Adjudication Committee)
Ideas received	496
Participation rate	84%
Ideas adopted	124
Success rate	25%
Total savings	£30,000
Highest award	£1,600
Other awards	Trophy for the most successful Division of the Company. An Ideas Club mug for the first award £30 and over. A badge giving membership of the Ideas Club for the first award.
Total awards	£5,070

INSPIRATIONS

History

Rolls-Royce Motor Cars introduced the scheme at Crewe in 1964 as a means to tap the resourcefulness of the workforce in a co-ordinated manner by giving them the opportunity to qualify for cash awards for their ideas. At this stage, however, only shop floor operatives were eligible to participate and it was not until 1979 that eligibility was extended to cover weekly staff. The scheme continued very successfully, although scheme administration believed that the full potential was not achieved.

This belief coupled with the company's policy to further enhance employee relations through harmonisation and involvement led among other things to a major cross functional review of the suggestion scheme during 1988, which resulted in a complete relaunch on January 1, 1989 under the new logo "Inspirations". The new scheme allows all employees to participate with the principle objective remaining "to encourage all employees to bring forward useful ideas which will benefit the company for which the employee may receive cash awards".

Organisation

The scheme operates for Rolls-Royce Motor Cars and also for the sister company Vickers Precision Components (VPC), which is sited within the Crewe complex and at Shrewsbury.

The main committee, who meet quarterly and are responsible for overseeing the operation, is comprised of the following Rolls-Royce Motor Car employees:

Director of Manufacturing Planning — Scheme Chair
Director of Current Engineering — Vice Chair

Manager Future Projects
Manager Quality Assurance
Manager Special Engines and Car Spares
Works Convenor — Employee Representative
Chief Estimator — Scheme Administrator

In addition, the Director of Manufacturing for VPC has a seat on the committee.

Scheme administration is conducted as part of the duties of the Chief Estimator, who employs two full-time investigators and a technical clerk.

To speed the evaluation process, a mini-committee meets quarterly comprising Scheme Administrator plus a Senior Planning Engineer together with an employee representative.

Ideas are assessed independently by Scheme Administration, who also request information from the appropriate department.

Marketing

Utilising its own independent identity, the workforce is reached through notice-boards, house magazines and monthly line briefings.

Special incentive exercises on specific subjects appear frequently, and notice is always taken of the "customer's" (suggestor's) expectations.

In fact a major part of the recent review was the response to a random survey of some 20% of the workforce, defining those customer expectations. Of course major consideration was given to the results when reforming the rules for our relaunch.

A presentation event is organised for major award winners with a ceremony in the boardroom. Special incentives award winners with either weekend holidays or goods such as TVs, cameras, etc.

Maximum publicity is gained for all major events using the company's Public Relations function, which extends also to local news media.

Allied to all this activity, the induction course run for new starters contains a sector totally dedicated to the scheme.

Basis of awards

Awards, up to the maximum of £5,000, are payable at 20% of expected savings based on full production rates over 12 months. No recourse to implementation costs are considered although approval for change is based on the full financial facts.

A points system which considers importance of change, application, and originality is utilised where monetary savings cannot be assessed.

Up to £25 can also be granted as encouragement awards, and the system of paying interim awards is also used.

Success stories

As you would expect from a scheme 25 years old, the success stories are many and varied. Particular significance must go to those showing major quality improvements on the best car in the world, such as redesigned headlamp wash/wipe system, redesigned head restraints and completely redesigned Bentley Turbo seats: all completed successfully using the suggestion scheme as a means of tapping the resource and ingenuity of the workforce. Being a manufacturing plant, Rolls Royce Motor Cars receives many ideas that increase the efficiency and utilisation of the plant, and we have also made significant improvements in power conservation.

As an additional bonus it has been most encouraging to note that talent has been recognised and in fact promotions have occurred due to the suggestion scheme.

Statistics

	1988	**First half of 1989**
Number of employees	4,683	4,700
Number eligible	3,718	4,700
Ideas received	455	895
Participation rate	12%	19%
Ideas adopted	120	245
Success rate	26%	27%
Total savings: direct	£420k	£100k
indirect	£60k	£20k
Total	£480k	£120k
Highest award (maximum)	£5,000	£5,000
Total awards	£39k	£18k

SUGGESTION SCHEME

History

The Suggestion Scheme at Barnard Castle was launched over 30 years ago. The emphasis of the scheme has always been staff involvement and performance improvement. From the company's point of view, financial consideration has always been secondary.

Organisation

The scheme is managed by a scheme manager and a small committee comprising a management representative, a trade union representative, and a management chair. Scheme manager is a permanent position; other appointments are for two years. The duty of the Suggestion Scheme Committee is to ensure that evaluations by departmental managers are fair and equitable and that the rules of the scheme are complied with. The committee is also responsible for promoting the scheme.

Basis of awards

Generally awards are based on 25% of the first year's gross savings. The evaluation is initially made by the manager of the department concerned, subsequently ratified by the Accounts manager, and given final approval by the Suggestion Scheme Committee.

Where a suggestion is not accepted, but the work involved in presenting the suggestion was meritorious, an encouragement gift may be made to the suggestor. This gift takes the form of a leather wallet, a pen and pencil set, a games compendium, etc.

Success story

The highest award we have ever made was £13,500 to Julia Fairish, an operator in our Cephalosporins Manufacturing Centre. This suggestion was placed first in the 1989 Industrial Society/UKASS Suggestion of the Year Competition – Technical Section.

Statistics for 1988

Number of employees	1,500
Employees eligible	1,500
Ideas received	340
Participation rate	22%
Ideas adopted	175
Success rate	50%
Total savings	N.A.
Total awards	£19,967

ON WINNING LINES

History

British Rail was formed on 1 January, 1948 from four major privately owned railway companies. Each of these ran its own suggestion scheme. The earliest of these was started by the Great Western Railway, way back in 1907, and the scheme has been in continual existence since then.

The scheme went through a major relaunch in 1988 when the whole process was overhauled. The regional committees, which were run on the lines of the former railway companies, were abandoned as was the manual operation of the scheme. The scheme has been centralised at York to look after the whole of the BR Network with the objective of maximising the good ideas from the workforce.

The overall objective is to provide a structured system where staff may make a contribution to improving the industry and for which they may receive a reward. Specifically, the participation rate is seen as an important measure of the success of the scheme.

A further objective is to generate financial benefits to the business whilst creating a cost-conscious workforce.

Organisation

The Staff Suggestions Unit is an entirely free-standing organisation of four people. The unit was located at York as this is central for the UK Operation. The Scheme Manager reports directly to the Managing Director (Operations and Engineering) who is second in line to the Chair. This is considered to be vital to give the scheme the credibility and support it needs within a large multi-functional business. There is no committee structure. After consideration it was decided that to form a committee would create delay without any real benefit. The awards are approved by both the Scheme

Manager and Scheme Co-ordination Officer for payments up to £10,000 and with the involvement of the Managing Director for awards in excess of this.

When ideas are received they are first given a code to identify any particular campaign. They then receive a title and the suggestor's manager and an evaluating officer are identified. The idea is entered into a computerised record which automatically allocates the next number and checks for the duplication of the idea. Acknowledgement letters are then sent to the suggestor; the target is for these to be sent on the day the suggestion is received. Next, evaluation takes place. Initially this is done by telephoning the evaluating officer. After discussion, the idea is either rejected; in which case a letter is sent to the suggestor, with or without an interest award, or the evaluating officer asks to see the suggestion in writing to give a full evaluation. The suggestion and evaluation form is then copied to the evaluator, and depending on the earlier comment, an interim award is paid.

The evaluator replies, and a target time of 21 days has been set, whereupon an award may be made. Frequently the idea has scope for wider application and thus the idea is sent to other evaluators. Evaluators are managers with ultimate responsibility in the function.

Marketing

The major relaunch of the scheme has been through the production of a video. This 15 minute production has been shown to staff at team briefings and the launch was accompanied by a personal visit of the scheme manager to all managers.

In addition to the video, leaflets which include a submission form are sent to every member of staff once a quarter plus an advertisement in the house magazine *Rail News* every month.

Tours of different locations are undertaken by members of the team and a large owl is erected and presentations made to the staff. A photo album of good ideas is kept for staff to look through together with a supply of entry forms.

An annual suggestion of the year competition is held at which the different rail businesses — Railfreight, InterCity, Provincial, Network South East and Parcels — each award a sector prize. The overall winner receives the Chairperson's Award.

Separate marketing ventures are used from time to time, ranging from the lucky draw to an extra prize awarded to all the winners in certain categories.

Each new suggestor is presented with a token award with their first acknowledgement letter. This is only a small item but is aimed at stimulating discussion in the workplace.

Basis of awards

Awards are based on 20% of the net benefit. If ideas have a high initial set-up cost, the annual savings are averaged over five years with a view to making the award fairer to the suggestor. Non-cash awards as mentioned above are made at the time of initial submission of the first idea. Additionally the awards of special prizes can be on the non-cash basis and microwave cookers have been given for energy saving ideas.

Success stories

Since our relaunch we have had many success stories, highlights of which are described below.

An increase in participation rate from 1.1% to 4.0%, with 36% of ideas receiving an award reflecting their merit compared to 25% previously. Savings in the first year have been in excess of £5 million, mainly due to some excellent winning lines.

We have been successful in being shortlisted in the Industrial Society UKASS competition in 1988 and in 1989. In 1989 we achieved a shortlisted entry in each of the three categories.

The greatest successes have flowed not just from the large number of ideas that have been submitted since the relaunch but in the positive approach many suggestors now have and the feedback we have received from them.

The signing of a certificate by the Managing Director which is presented to the author(s) of each adopted suggestion is just one of the ways that every local manager has become more involved in the scheme. It has brought the scheme closer to the staff that it is aimed at, and now many local managers are writing articles to encourage ideas from their staff. The Managing Director hosts lunch for major winners and their spouses approximately monthly.

Statistics for 1988

Number of employees	130,857
Employees eligible	130,857
Ideas received	5,234
Participation rate	4%
Ideas adopted	471
Success rate	9%
Total savings	£5.5 million
Highest award	£20,000 (limit £25,000)
Total awards	£120,000

STAFF SUGGESTIONS SCHEME

History

The Lloyds Bank Scheme was established in 1968 to stimulate new ideas. The Scheme strives to communicate effectively with all staff and thereby motivate them towards a rewarding flow of quality ideas of immediate benefit to the bank and to the successful individuals.

Organisation

The Scheme is an integral part of the bank's structure and is given support from the highest level. The Committee comprises a General Manager, Head of Banking Department, Regional General Manager and a Senior Branch Manager, striving to achieve a clear understanding of each type of suggestion, including the following wider implications.

1. To consider the implications and prospects of all suggestions in the wider context of future developments and initiatives, obtaining the relevant policy decision when appropriate.
2. To quantify as accurately as possible in financial terms the benefit to the bank arising directly from the suggestions being made.
3. To relate awards for suggestions as closely as practicable to tangible and quantified benefits to the bank.
4. To provide for the reward of some suggestions which have merit, but which for various reasons cannot be implemented.
5. To report results in a suitable form for communication to both the executive and staff, including for the former a "Profit and Loss" Statement.

The Committee, through the Suggestions Secretary, seeks the views of the relevant Divisions or Departments upon the merits of the original suggestion, and requests up-to-date comment on some duplicate proposals. The Secretary will ask for quantification, as accurately as practicable, of the value of all suggestions which have been accepted and brief reasons for those that have been rejected. The Secretary will report to the Committee the best possible estimate of the benefit to the bank of suggestions recommended for an award, in accordance with the scheme's guidelines.

Marketing

All new staff of the bank are advised about the Suggestions Scheme and are given our Brochure "Turn Your Good Ideas Into Cash", which describes the objects of the Scheme, how to submit ideas, and which areas would not be eligible for submissions.

Additionally, every member of the staff receives a copy of the monthly internal newspaper *Lloyds Bank News*, which carries regular items on the Scheme, together with a list of the award winners and the subject that the ideas cover.

The Scheme is conscious of the need to continue to promote good ideas and new incentives are being planned in this area to stimulate further growth. A recent monthly campaign in March was used to generate ideas to improve branch routines which would assist in our extended opening period. The support of this was excellent with 520 suggestions received during the period. Current trends for this year project that the number of suggestions we receive for 1989 should be double the previous year which has resulted from a higher exposure to staff of the Scheme.

Basis of awards

In order that a suitable Award may be identified and approved by the Committee, suggestions are allocated to one of four categories.

Savings confirmed

Where the relative Division/Department accept the suggestion and have felt able to ascribe an annual saving figure, awards will be based upon 10% of the first year's saving.

Savings unquantified or unquantifiable — but significant

The appropriate award for a saving in this category is £200 and the significant aspect must be confirmed by the relevant department.

Savings unquantified or unquantifiable — but nominal

Into this category fall those suggestions which are implemented but whose value is problematical to assess or very small. The department concerned normally confirms that a small saving exists. It is considered appropriate to nominate an Award of £100.

Goodwill awards

This category covers two types of suggestions. Those which provide no tangible benefits, i.e. cosmetic amendments to standard forms. Secondly, it covers those having merit even though for various reasons they cannot be implemented, i.e. where a presentation, or the time and effort spent deserves recognition.

Award numbers continue to rise and last year's awards of £37,150 shared by 183 winners was an all time record for the Scheme. This year, if the present trend continues, it looks like these figures will be overtaken by the present impetus of new ideas.

UK Statistics for 1988

Number of employees	60,000
Employees eligible	60,000
Ideas received	3,469
Participation rate	6%
Ideas adopted	183
Success rate	5.4%
Total savings	£306,505
Highest award	£4,000
Total awards	£37,150

APPENDICES

THE UNITED KINGDOM ASSOCIATION OF SUGGESTION SCHEMES

The United Kingdom Association of Suggestion Schemes (UKASS) was launched in May 1987 by The Industrial Society at a conference attended by some 150 representatives of companies and public sector organisations, all of whom were interested either in launching new schemes or improving ones which already existed.

The idea of getting together to form an Association came about as a direct result of the considerable national interest aroused by a series of four programmes about suggestion schemes which appeared on BBC Television in the Autumn of 1986 under the title of "Ideas Unlimited". The series was developed by the BBC in consultation with The Industrial Society, and it reviewed schemes in the UK and elsewhere in the world, identifying some of the secrets of success and getting the views of the suggestors themselves as well as those of top executives and scheme co-ordinators. The final programme featured competitions for the best company schemes and for the best individual idea.

At the end of the series, there were numerous enquiries for further information and this lead naturally to the first conference and the launch of the Association. UKASS is dedicated to demonstrating the benefits of good ideas, encouraging the establishment of well-run schemes, and providing a forum for advice and for the exchange of views.

In the first two years of its existence a membership of over 500 organisations has been achieved by the Association, which continues to benefit from advice and administrative support provided by The Industrial Society. Up to six training seminars are held each year with The Industrial Society in different parts of the country and a quarterly newsletter is published. The main event, however, is the Annual Conference to which both scheme co-ordinators and winning suggestors are invited. Apart from presentations and workshops the programme includes a social dinner and a competition for winning ideas in three categories (technical, internal services, and customer service). Presentations are made to the winners in each category and there is a trophy and special prize for the overall winner. Since the competition was reintroduced it has continued to be featured in a BBC programme.

As a measure of the potential benefits which can result from good ideas, the Association estimates that savings of £300 million per annum are achievable in the United Kingdom. The primary benefits, however, will continue to be improved teamwork and commitment from the workforce.

On the wider scene, strong links are being forged with Associations in many other countries and it is planned that an International Association will be launched at a conference in London in 1990.

How The Industrial Society and UKASS can help you:

Information: We have a collection of suggestion scheme literature, including guidelines, forms and posters.

Advice: We can visit you and help you launch or revitalise your scheme.

Training: We regularly run seminars and workshops in which successful scheme managers explain their schemes and offer practical advice.

Publications: We sell suggestions scheme surveys, information packs and a new book and video *Ideas Unlimited: how to run a successful suggestion scheme.*

For further information contact Jean Balcombe or Cathy Burroughs at the following address:

The Information Service
The Industrial Society
48 Bryanston Square
London W1H 7LN

Telephone: 01-262 2401

EXTRA STATUTORY CONCESSION: SUGGESTION SCHEMES

Income tax will not be charged under Schedule E in respect of an award made by an employer to an employee under a Staff Suggestion Scheme where the following conditions are satisfied:

a. There is a formally constituted scheme under which suggestions are made and it is open to all employees on equal terms.

b. The suggestion for which the award is made is outside the scope of the employee's normal duties. The test is whether, taking account of his experience, the employee could not reasonably have been expected to have put forward such a suggestion as part of the duties of his post. Where meetings of employees are held for the purpose of putting forward suggestions, they should be regarded as part of their duties and any consequential awards would not be within the terms of this concession.

c. Awards other than encouragement awards (see g) are only made following a decision to implement the suggestion and are made directly to the employees concerned.

d. The decision to make an award other than an encouragement award is based on the degree of improvement in efficiency and/or effectiveness likely to be achieved measured by reference to:
   - the prospective financial benefits and the period over which they would accrue and
   - the importance of the subject matter having regard to the nature of the employer's business.

e. The amount of an award does not exceed:

- 50 per cent of the expected net financial benefit during the first year of implementation or
- 10 per cent of the expected net financial benefit over a period of up to 5 years.

subject to an overriding maximum of £5,000. Where an award exceeds £5,000 the excess is not covered by this concession.

f. Where a suggestion is put forward by more than one employee the award made under (e) above is divided between them on a reasonable basis.

g. Any encouragement award is of £25 or less. An encouragement award is one which is made in respect of a suggestion which, though it will not be implemented, has some intrinsic merit and/or reflects meritorious effort on the part of the employee in making the suggestion.

This concession does not apply to any liability to income tax or capital gains tax on income or gains arising from the exploitation or disposal of rights in an invention devised by the employee, eg patent rights, know-how etc.*

*Inland Revenue Guidelines on suggestion schemes were published in 1988. The Industrial Society and UKASS advise organisations to consult with the appropriate Tax Office on specific interpretation and application.

PATENTS AND COPYRIGHT

Patents

The Law relating to Patent, Design and Copyright is a subject that is well worthwhile obtaining legal advice upon if an idea is likely to fall into this area. It is important to note, however, that the cost involved in Patents can be considerable and alternative ways can be used to protect others from obtaining a Patent if the idea is unlikely to be exploited externally.

Whilst this book is not intended to give a detailed explanation of the law relating to Patent and Copyright — it would involve a book of similar size to this one to do that — it is worthwhile mentioning the implication of the law as it relates to suggestion schemes.

The main Patent Law is contained in the 1977 Act with limited amendments in the 1986 and 1988 Acts. For our purposes it is worth noting that a Patent may be granted only for an invention which:

i is new
ii involves an inventive step
iii is capable of industrial application.

Patents cannot be granted for:

i a discovery, scientific theory or mathematical method
ii a literary, dramatic, musical or artistic work or any aesthetic creation whatsoever
iii a scheme, rule or method for performing a mental act, playing a game or doing business, or a program for a computer
iv a presentation of information

v an invention, the publication or exploitation of which would be generally expected to encourage offensive, immoral or anti-social behaviour
vi for any variety of animal or plant or any essentially biological process for the production of animals or plants, not being a micro biological process or the product of such a process.

The important point to remember is that if the product or process is known about prior to the date of application either by written or oral description in the UK or elsewhere, then it may not be considered as an invention and as a result may not be patented.

The application for a patent may be made by:

i the inventor(s)
ii a person(s) who had an agreement with the inventor prior to him/her making the invention
iii the successor to the title.

Separate sections of the 1977 Act are devoted to employees' inventions and these state that the invention shall belong to the employer if:

i it was made in the course of duties or in the course of duties falling outside normal duties but specially assigned to him/her and the circumstances in either case were such that the invention might reasonably be expected to result from the carrying out of his/her duties, or
ii the invention was made in the course of the duties of the employee and at the time of making the invention because of the nature of his/her duties and the particular responsibilities arising from the nature of his/her duties he/she had special obligation to further the interests of the employer's undertaking.

Any invention made by the employee shall as between him/her and his/her employer be taken for those purposes to belong to the employee. Special arrangements within the Act provide for compensation to the employee for an invention. This outlines what should be taken into account and provides for any benefit already derived to the employee. The points to consider are:

i effort and skill of the employee
ii assistance from other employees
iii contribution of the employer, e.g. provision of opportunity
iv nature of duties.

Near the end of the section dealing with employees' inventions a paragraph states:

> Any term in a contract (including a contract of employment) which diminishes the employees' rights in the inventions of any description made by him/her after the appointed day and date of the contract should be unenforceable against him/her to the extent that it diminishes those rights.

To patent any invention is a very expensive process, especially if the patent is applied for in many countries. The patent also has to be renewed each year to remain valid and this too can be costly. An idea can be protected by publishing details of it. This will clearly prevent any other organisation from patenting it, although it will not prevent it using it.

Design rights

Design Right Law was established under the 1988 Act which replaced the provisions of the 1968 Design Copyright Act. Design Right is non-registrable and may coexist with copyright or design registration. To enact Design Right, a drawing, written description or other representation of the industrial design should be signed by or on behalf of the originator and dated. Design Right applies to the design of any aspect of the shape or configuration of the article, its whole or part of it, external or internal.

The owner of Design Right has an exclusive right to make articles exactly or substantially to the design, and an infringement is actionable, by the Design Right owner.

Registered design

The 1949 Act allowed certain designs to be registered for 15 years. Under that Act the only designs that are allowed registration are those judged by eye, not dictated by function. The 1988 Act makes minor amendments to the existing legislation and whilst removing some designs from the registration, where the design of the part is determined by the whole, it extends the period of protection from 15 to 25 years.

Copyright

Copyright is based on the Berne Convention of 1886 and the Universal

Copyright convention of 1952. This has been chaged by British Law, most recently by the 1988 Act.

Copyright gives legal rights to the creators of certain kinds of material so that they can control the various ways in which their material may be exploited. All literary, dramatic, musical and artistic works, published editions of works, sound recordings, films, broadcasts, and computer programs are protected and the material does not need to have novelty or aesthetic value.

Whilst a work may be protected, the idea behind it is not. A name or title may not be protected by copyright.

Copyright does not need to be registered, so there are no fees to pay. Whilst in the UK the work does not need to be marked this is not the case in every country and notably in the USA it is a legal requirement to mark the material with the international symbol ©.*

*The Industrial Society and UKASS disclaim any responsibility for matters of fact or interpretation and advise organisations to seek independent legal advice on all matters, general or specific.